CHOSEN

JORDAN M. RIEDEL

Copyright 2020 Jordan M. Riedel

ALL RIGHTS RESERVED. This book contains material protected under International and Federal Copyright Laws and Treaties. Any unauthorized reprint or use of this material is prohibited. No part of this book may be reproduced or transmitted in any form or by any means, electronic or mechanical, including photocopying, recording, or by any information storage and retrieval system without express written permission from the author/publisher.

ISBN: 978-1-64184-468-0 (paperback)
ISBN: 978-1-64184-467-3 (hardback)
ISBN: 978-1-64184-469-7 (eBook)

Dedication

First and foremost, this message is dedicated to God. Thank you for sending your Son, Jesus Christ, to die on the cross, that I may be saved.

Also, I would like to dedicate this to my beautiful wife, Natalie. God has truly given me more than I could have ever asked for in our marriage. You are such a blessing to me. Thank you for putting up with all my time at the computer writing for hours on end. I love you.

And to my and Natalie's children. One, we will get to meet at a later time in Heaven, and our two sons, Tyler Preston and Henry Callen, who we get to enjoy time with here on Earth. May God bless their lives, that they may follow the one true God.

To my parents Mike and Rhonda Riedel, for raising me up in the church and teaching me how to have a relationship with the one true God.

TABLE OF CONTENTS

Introduction vii

The Opening 1

Judas Iscariot 8

The Paths 26

Choosing to Follow God 52

The True Mystery of God's Plan 64

Choose to be Chosen 71

The Last Chapter 107

INTRODUCTION

For the entirety of the "After Death" era—or whatever people call it now to be politically correct—two specific questions have been raised: "Who was Judas Iscariot?" and "Why did he betray Jesus Christ?" Growing up in the church, I frequently asked myself these questions. I couldn't and still cannot understand why Judas, one of the twelve disciples, one of Jesus Christ's main followers in his ministry on Earth, and his well-known friend, turned away from his teachings so drastically that he traded Jesus' life for 40 pieces of silver. In doing so, he was, and still is, labeled as one of the most deceptive people of all time. The Bible tells us in Romans 3:23 (KJV), *"For all have sinned and come short of the glory of God."* But what drives a man who is devoted to a cause (in this case, devoted to the Son of God Himself), to turn on it only for the sake of money? Like any problem, there has to be a root cause behind his methods and thinking.

God has put it on my heart to write about two characters from the Bible—Judas Iscariot and the Apostle Paul. Judas Iscariot is the man who betrayed Jesus, as all the apostles will remind us, and keep reminding us throughout the scripture. The Apostle Paul is known for killing Christians of the early church, and then changing his life around to follow the teachings of Jesus, writing approximately two thirds of the New Testament scripture. They were two drastically different men with two drastically different purposes in life. I have always been the kind of guy to believe that free will is something we have and something that can never be taken away from us. The Bible gives many examples of God giving man freedom to choose. Some examples are:

Genesis 2:16-17 (NIV) *"¹⁶ And the LORD God commanded the man, "You are free to eat from any tree in the garden; ¹⁷ but you must not eat from the tree of knowledge of good and evil, for when you eat from it you certainly die."*

John 1:12-13 (NIV) *"¹² Yet to all who did receive him, to those who believed in his name, he gave the right to become children of God—¹³ children born not of natural descent, nor of human decision or a husband's will, but born of God."*

Revelation 3:14-20 (NIV) *"¹⁴ To the angel of the church in Laodicea write: These are the words of the Amen, the faithful and true witness, the ruler of God's creation. ¹⁵ I know your deeds, that you are neither cold nor hot. I wish you were either one or the other! ¹⁶ So, because you are lukewarm—neither hot nor cold—I am about to spit you out of my mouth. ¹⁷ You say, 'I am rich; I have acquired wealth and do not need a thing.' But you do not realize that you are wretched, pitiful, poor, blind and naked. ¹⁸ I counsel you to buy from me gold refined in the fire, so you can become rich; and white clothes to wear, so you can cover your shameful nakedness; and salve to put on your eyes, so you can see. ¹⁹ Those whom I love I rebuke and discipline. So be earnest and repent. ²⁰ Here I am! I stand at the door and knock. If anyone hears my voice and opens the door, I will come in and eat with that person, and they with me."*

Of course, there are many more examples within the Bible. The Bible also pushes back on free will to some extent. It makes it almost seem that God has predestined some individuals to be His Chosen or Elect. There are some verses given that allude to this thought:

Proverbs 16:9 (NIV) *"In their hearts humans plan their course, but the Lord establishes their steps."*

John 15:16-17 (NIV) *"¹⁶ You did not choose me, but I chose you and appointed you so that you might go and bear fruit—fruit that will last—and so that whatever you ask in my name the Father will give you. ¹⁷ This is my command: Love each other."*

Ephesians 1:11–12 (NIV) *"¹¹ In him we were also chosen, having been predestined according to the plan of him who works out everything in conformity with the purpose of his will, ¹² in order that we, who were the first to put our hope in Christ, might be for the praise of his glory."*

1 Peter 1:1–2 (NIV) *"¹ Peter, an apostle of Jesus Christ, To God's elect, exiles scattered throughout the provinces of Pontus, Galatia, Cappadocia, Asia and Bithynia, ² who have been chosen according to the foreknowledge of God the Father, through the sanctifying work of the Spirit, to be obedient to Jesus Christ and sprinkled with his blood: Grace and peace be yours in abundance."*

In the simplest terms, it may seem that God had chosen His followers before they even stepped forth on the earth. By these verses, it almost seems that He has predetermined individuals to fulfill His plans. I know what you are thinking. "Wow, Jordan, so you're telling me that it doesn't matter if I try to believe in God, He has already chosen people to be with Him for all eternity?" Or, "Why should I even try to follow God if I, like Judas, am destined to fail?" There have been times in my life where I have thrown up my hands and asked God the same questions. I still, to this day, ask the same questions. I am a cut-and-dry type of person. I am a very visual person. In a lot of things I do, if I can't see it, I truly don't believe it and have doubts about it, whatever it may be. I have loved God my entire life, and I whole-heartedly believe He has never left me throughout any life circumstance and never will. I know I am one of God's Elect or Appointed. I simply question, "What about those who are not?" and "If someone is destined to fail in life, do I, Jordan Michael Riedel, have the ability to change that?" As a Christian, the Bible tells me I must do my best to witness to others about Jesus and how he shed his blood for our sins, as a living sacrifice for all mankind. But if someone is destined to spend eternity in Hell, is it possible to change the will God has for their life and turn them to the one true God, see them truly repent, and become part of God's chosen people?

I have faith that the God I serve, the one true God, in His all-powerful ways, can influence humans' hearts and minds. Likewise, so can Satan, the father of lies. There is no gauge on the point of no return for the human mind and heart. I believe it is different for each individual. Is there a point in time when the opportunity of choice has diminished, and one is eternally damned? Surely not. So what is the answer? I believe through this study, all of us will find answers—the answers God would have us find.

I encourage you to pray on the messages God has given me while you are reading this. If you are not a Christian and you're not too sure about some of these beliefs—or theories, if you will—then dig into them for yourself. Don't take my words as perfect, for I am simply a human being (imperfect). Though my intentions are pure, this is not the Bible, and do not take these words as such. I will use scripture to validate a point of study in some cases. My purpose for writing this is to glorify God the Father, God the Son, and God the Holy Spirit. By the end of this, I hope you believe as I believe, and hope as I hope. Over all that is spoken, my hope and prayer for you is to find the one true God, the way you are supposed to find Him, and not by my limited knowledge. My hope for you is to, if not already, become one of the chosen people of God.

1
THE OPENING

From the time I was a child, I have had many questions about life. Why are we here? What is my purpose in life? Why do bad things happen to good people? You know, the types of questions every child asks and some, if not all, adults may as well. The Bible tells us that each person has a purpose and that God has a plan for our lives. I believe this concept wholeheartedly. The most recent question God has placed on my heart is this: "Is this 'destiny' of mine already determined, or can I control it?"

It's a known fact that people struggle with change, but if you knew that no matter what you did, your life was already predetermined, would you act differently? In studying this topic, my mindset has changed drastically from *I can control everything I do and am involved in* to *I can control everything I do, but there will always be factors in this world I can't control.* I will forever be in a reactionary position. Life is all about how we react to the things around us. Personally, I try to plan and plan and plan, sometimes to the point of driving myself and those around me nuts. I like and appreciate perfect order. I'm not insane; at least I don't think I am. I may be a little (or a lot) OCD, but I am the way God made me, so I have learned to accept that and work through my struggles the best that I can. Regardless of how we want things to turn out in life, we can't control everything. We can't control God's plan. This world is full of things we cannot control, but God can.

Let's take sickness and death, for instance. The Bible tells us that death entered into the world when Adam and Eve sinned, for the first time in human history, in the Garden of Eden. With death came ways to die; things that were and are out of human control. Things that were and are out of my control. One of the most difficult ideas for me to grasp throughout my life has been good people getting sick or good people dying earlier than expected. Why would God send us to Earth to live for a short while and then die? In my simple mind, I don't have a good answer to this question. Yes, it bothers me; I am not the only one it bothers. We all struggle to find our purpose. The Bible says, "Seek and you will find." Sometimes that means we need to keep seeking and keep seeking and keep seeking. But things happen for a reason, right? We don't always understand or fully comprehend why things happen or why people do what they do. We don't always have the luxury of finding out the answers to all of life's questions. Even when we keep seeking, we don't always receive the answer. For some of us, our purpose is to keep seeking (God, of course). For others, you know your specific purpose in life. You have always known your purpose. You will fulfill that purpose at all costs. And you will die with that purpose.

In my life, I look to God and the Bible for answers to life's questions. The answer the Bible gives is not always clear-cut; t's not always black and white. Hence, I keep seeking. When God gives me clear direction, I know because it aligns with what the Bible says. To be honest, sometimes, God does not give me a clear answer (I know I'm not alone in this). I think the answer to a question like "Why do bad things happen to good people?" is "Because it does…that's life." That is just life, and we all have to find a way to deal with it. Not to be morbid, but we only have to deal with it until we die. Then, and only then, will we find out how we lived our lives. We will be in Heaven, or we will be in Hell. Depending on how we lived our lives, we will find ourselves basking in the glory of God for the rest of time, or eternally damned to a lake of fire. Apologies for being so blunt and dark, but life isn't always cupcakes and roses. Parts of this message are going to be straightforwardly honest and raw.

There have been many stories throughout history of people finding their purpose in life. One of my favorites is the story of the Apostle Paul. The Bible tells us of a man named Saul.

(I have a quick side note: For those of you reading this and do not believe in God, I believe this message is for you, too. So please take the Bible as a historical reference for now and don't give up on reading this because I reference it so much. By the end, I hope to change your perspective about the Bible and God, in general.)

Anyway, back to it. Saul. The Bible tells us of a man named Saul, also known as the Apostle Paul. The backstory is that Saul was a Jew who was killing Christians at the time (the time of the early Christian Church). And we'll just say for simplistic reasons: God didn't like that.

In Acts 9:1-31(NIV), God changed that: *"¹ Meanwhile, Saul was still breathing out murderous threats against the Lord's disciples. He went to the high priest ² and asked him for letters to the synagogues in Damascus, so that if he found any there who belonged to the Way, whether men or women, he might take them as prisoners to Jerusalem. ³ As he neared Damascus on his journey, suddenly a light from heaven flashed around him. ⁴ He fell to the ground and heard a voice say to him, 'Saul, Saul, why do you persecute me?'*

⁵ 'Who are you, Lord?' Saul asked.

'I am Jesus, whom you are persecuting,' he replied. ⁶ 'Now get up and go into the city, and you will be told what you must do.'

⁷ The men traveling with Saul stood there speechless; they heard the sound but did not see anyone. ⁸ Saul got up from the ground, but when he opened his eyes he could see nothing. So they led him by the hand into Damascus. ⁹ For three days he was blind, and did not eat or drink anything.

¹⁰ In Damascus there was a disciple named Ananias. The Lord called to him in a vision, 'Ananias!'

'Yes, Lord,' he answered.

¹¹ The Lord told him, 'Go to the house of Judas on Straight Street and ask for a man from Tarsus named Saul, for he is praying. ¹² In a vision he has seen a man named Ananias come and place his hands on him to restore his sight.'

[13] 'Lord,' Ananias answered, 'I have heard many reports about this man and all the harm he has done to your holy people in Jerusalem. [14] And he has come here with authority from the chief priests to arrest all who call on your name.'

[15] But the Lord said to Ananias, 'Go! This man is my chosen instrument to proclaim my name to the Gentiles and their kings and to the people of Israel. [16] I will show him how much he must suffer for my name.'

[17] Then Ananias went to the house and entered it. Placing his hands on Saul, he said, 'Brother Saul, the Lord—Jesus, who appeared to you on the road as you were coming here—has sent me so that you may see again and be filled with the Holy Spirit.' [18] Immediately, something like scales fell from Saul's eyes, and he could see again. He got up and was baptized, [19] and after taking some food, he regained his strength. Saul spent several days with the disciples in Damascus. [20] At once he began to preach in the synagogues that Jesus is the Son of God. [21] All those who heard him were astonished and asked, 'Isn't he the man who raised havoc in Jerusalem among those who call on this name? And hasn't he come here to take them as prisoners to the chief priests?' [22] Yet Saul grew more and more powerful and baffled the Jews living in Damascus by proving that Jesus is the Messiah.

[23] After many days had gone by, there was a conspiracy among the Jews to kill him, [24] but Saul learned of their plan. Day and night they kept close watch on the city gates in order to kill him. [25] But his followers took him by night and lowered him in a basket through an opening in the wall.

[26] When he came to Jerusalem, he tried to join the disciples, but they were all afraid of him, not believing that he really was a disciple. [27] But Barnabas took him and brought him to the apostles. He told them how Saul on his journey had seen the Lord and that the Lord had spoken to him, and how in Damascus he had preached fearlessly in the name of Jesus. [28] So Saul stayed with them and moved about freely in Jerusalem, speaking boldly in the name of the Lord. [29] He talked and debated with the Hellenistic Jews, but they tried to kill

him. *³⁰ When the believers learned of this, they took him down to Caesarea and sent him off to Tarsus.*

³¹ Then the church throughout Judea, Galilee and Samaria enjoyed a time of peace and was strengthened. Living in the fear of the Lord and encouraged by the Holy Spirit, it increased in numbers."

Paul went on to be a founder of the "Gentile" Christian Church. He paved the way for many to find Jesus Christ as their Lord and Savior. This was all made possible by one occurrence on the Road to Damascus. Paul, I believe, lays out his life's purpose in Ephesians 3:2-6 (NIV): *"² Surely you have heard about the administration of God's grace that was given to me for you, ³ that is, the mystery made known to me by revelation, as I have already written briefly. ⁴ In reading this, then, you will be able to understand my insight into the mystery of Christ, ⁵ which was not made known to people in other generations as it has now been revealed by the Spirit to God's holy apostles and prophets. ⁶ This mystery is that through the gospel the Gentiles are heirs together with Israel, members together of one body, and sharers together in the promise in Christ Jesus."*

Paul had it pretty easy. One day, he was killing Christians, and the next week, he was leading people to Christ, all because Jesus showed him His will in a flash of light. Now, there are probably not a lot of us out there killing Christians in the way that Paul was, but we all do or have done things we are not proud of in our lives. Everyone doesn't always have a "Road to Damascus" type of experience to come to know Christ. Most of the time, a change in a person's life doesn't occur with "a flash", nor are there any bright lights—it will likely be a little bit more subtle. On the other hand, oftentimes, people do not see the opportunity or reason to change. Whatever the reason is (and there could be many), they simply do not change and/or do not want to change.

Now for the second character of the Bible to discuss. I'm sure you all have an inkling of who Judas Iscariot was from hearing the Easter story, year after year. Paul, on the other hand, some may not know. You have read a little about him thus far and will continue to read about him if you choose to continue to read this message. Some days you are going to be like Judas, and some days you're going to be like Paul. Regardless of who you are portraying at any given moment, you have the opportunity to be with God and His followers throughout eternity. You have the opportunity to be God's Elect. Either way you choose, God will use you. It simply depends on if you want to go to Heaven or Hell. Out of the two men this message is about, one will be in Heaven (Paul), and the other will be in Hell (Judas).

In Matthew 22:1-14 (ESV), Jesus describes the Kingdom of Heaven in this way: *"¹ And again Jesus spoke to them in parables, saying, ² "The kingdom of heaven may be compared to a king who gave a wedding feast for his son, ³ and sent his servants to call those who were invited to the wedding feast, but they would not come. ⁴ Again he sent other servants, saying, 'Tell those who are invited, "See, I have prepared my dinner, my oxen and my fat calves have been slaughtered, and everything is ready. Come to the wedding feast."' ⁵ But they paid no attention and went off, one to his farm, another to his business, ⁶ while the rest seized his servants, treated them shamefully, and killed them. ⁷ The king was angry, and he sent his troops and destroyed those murderers and burned their city. ⁸ Then he said to his servants, 'The wedding feast is ready, but those invited were not worthy. ⁹ Go therefore to the main roads and invite to the wedding feast as many as you find.' ¹⁰ And those servants went out into the roads and gathered all whom they found, both bad and good. So the wedding hall was filled with guests. ¹¹ "But when the king came in to look at the guests, he saw there a man who had no wedding garment. ¹² And he said to him, 'Friend, how did you get in here without a wedding garment?' And he was speechless. ¹³ Then the king said to the attendants, 'Bind him hand and foot and cast him into the outer darkness. In that place there will be weeping and gnashing of teeth.' ¹⁴ For many are called, but few are chosen."*

This parable that Jesus gives us has a grave distinction between being called and being chosen. Simply put, one can be called, but may or may not be chosen. The acceptance into the Kingdom of Heaven is being chosen by God, not necessarily, the calling. For instance, say two persons (they could be male or female) are called to go to the Olympics. These two persons are of equal build, stature, physical ability in their event, etc. The only difference is one is chosen by God to win, and the other is not. Say they are sprinters, and they are neck and neck down to the last 10 meters of a 100-meter race because they are equal in all attributes. Then one trips and falls to the ground, and the other finishes. They were both called to be in that race at that time, seeing that it takes a certain person with the right training and ability to get to that level of a running career, but due to a minor glitch in one's form, a moist spot on the track, or some other form of random occurrence the one that tripped lost the race, and the person that finished, won. The winner was chosen to win the race. We do not always have a choice to change fate. So how do we become called and/or chosen?

Judas Iscariot was called by God. He met that call to follow Jesus for approximately three years or so. I would submit to you that he was not chosen. He was not a chosen child of God. Of course, this is all based on the observation that he turned Jesus over to be executed. If that doesn't qualify a person as "getting into the wedding with no wedding garment," I'm not sure what does. But was he called to betray Jesus or chosen to betray him? I submit to you he was called but not chosen, and it was his own selfish ambition that caused him to give up being chosen. It was his choice to fall short.

2

JUDAS ISCARIOT

The Origins of Judas Iscariot

It's funny how some things trickle through time. Certain historical moments change the world as we know it, and others (the majority of others) dwindle away as if they never happened. It's nothing we can control as human beings; it's all about perspective. It's all about how one sees the world and what is important to that individual. For instance, to me, the birth of Jesus Christ was the most important date in history. I grew up in the church, and I attended church throughout my entire adult life. I believe that God gave his one and only son, Jesus Christ, as a living sacrifice for the sake of mankind, and through Him, my sins are forgiven. I believe in the Holy Trinity and love them as the deity I serve. I believe they are the one God of this world, and all others are false. But, from a worldly perspective, others believe in other things. To them, the birth of Christ may mean nothing because He is not their savior and redeemer. They may serve another god or no god at all. It's all about perspective.

After looking at many references, the birthplace of Judas Iscariot was never captured in any legitimate historical reference. His birthplace can only be assumed. There is no factual content, only assumptions made from historians and theologians. For some reason—I'm pretty sure no one will ever really know the truth—this moment was not captured in history. No one during that time said, "This is an important moment. I'm going to write this down so that people from generation to generation can look back and remember this." The moment was lost in time, and the only logical reason that comes to my mind in thinking of why it was never recorded is, in the grand scheme of things, it really doesn't matter where he was born.

The origins of Judas Iscariot are unknown. A historical recording of his childhood, teenaged years, and the beginning of his adult life does not exist. The Bible does not mention anything of Judas' life, besides his father's name, who was Simon Iscariot. The Apostle John captures Judas being the son of Simon Iscariot three separate times (John 6:71, John 13:2, and John 13:26). In all of my research (I spent a total of about three hours looking into this, performing extensive Google searches, so please don't think I'm an expert on the topic), I was able to identify two common philosophies about Judas Iscariot and his life previous to following Jesus. I only spent about three hours researching it because I feel like if it was something worthwhile to research, someone would have taken the time to write a little bit more about the topic throughout the 2,000 years of history between then and now.

According to the article *Judas Iscariot*, by Kevin Knight, the origins of Judas Iscariot are not given in the Bible. The beginnings of Judas' life are not described in the Bible. The article goes on to explain Judas' place of birth. It also describes the meaning of the name Judas as, "Judas (Ioudas) is the Greek form of Judah (Hebrew 'praised')." It also gives an indication that Judas, based on his surname "Iscariot," could have been born in a city of Judah, called Kerioth or Carioth.

The *Encyclopedia Britannica* has a section titled "Judas Iscariot; Apostle." The article mentions that Judas' surname "Iscariot" is "probably a corruption of the Latin term 'sicarius,' meaning murderer, or assassin." The article also indicates that "Iscariot" would have meant Judas came from a group called the "Sicarii." The Sicarii were a group of radical Jews. In his book, *The Journal of Religion,* Richard A. Horsley discussed the Sicarii (Sicarioi). He describes them as an ancient Jewish Terrorist group, which in 66–70 A.D. tried to overthrow Rome. The Sicarii were part of a liberation that was organized by them and a couple of other nationalistic radical groups.

As we can tell, one theory about Judas' upbringing gives us a location where he could have been from originally. Shot in the dark. The other gives the terrorist group he may or may not have been a part of. Just another way to look at a shot in the dark. As to how credible these sources may be, the world will never know (but honestly, do they care?). Throughout history, the mysterious story of Judas has also brought forms of the second part of history (a story). If you have not heard of it before, there is a "Gospel of Judas," and just to be clear, the "Gospel of Judas" is not found in the Bible. The article *FAQs: Judas Iscariot "What the Four Canonical Gospels Say about the Notorious Apostle"* describes the "Gospel of Judas" as being found in El Minya, Egypt, in the 1970s. It says it was in "fragmentary form," and the document took a team of scholars many years to reconstruct and translate the document. The "Gospel of Judas" was released to the public in April of 2006. The article claims it to be a "Gnostic" text.

In short, the "Gospel of Judas" explains how Jesus came to Judas and asked him to betray Him. If Judas did this, he would have a guaranteed seat in Heaven. It even goes so far as to say he would be greater than the rest of the disciples in Heaven. It is a Gnostic text, meaning it is believed in or by a group, or sect, of people who also believe they have a higher spiritual knowledge than most. I'm not too sure the "Gospel of Judas" is a historical reference that can be trusted.

According to *The New World Encyclopedia*, in the article "Papias," Judas was given by Apostolic Father Papias, who preserved details of Judas' Death and other, should I say, strange details of Judas. The article also explains that Papias is, still to this day, known in some sects of the Orthodox and Catholic faiths as a saint and martyr, so most likely, his accounts are one of the more justifiable outside of the Bible, but still potentially in question. Also, the "why" of how he captured some details is still unclear. The authors of *The New World Encyclopedia* explained Papias' description of Judas in this way: "Judas walked about in this world a terrible example of impiety; his flesh swollen to such an extent that, where a wagon can pass with ease, he was not able to pass, no, not even the mass of his head merely. They say that his eyelids swelled to such an extent that he could not see the light at all, while as for his eyes they were not visible even by a physician looking through an instrument, so far had they sunk from the surface. His genital was larger and presented a more repugnant sight than has ever been seen; and through it there seeped from every part of the body a procession of pus and worms to his shame, even as he relieved himself (preserved by Apollinarius of Laodicea)."

For reference, I had to do about 30 more minutes of research for this one (and I believe this gentleman did a tad bit more research than me on the topic; his thesis on the Death of Judas is 228 pages long). According to Jesse Robertson, Ph.D. (and he earned it by writing this one), "Papias refers to Judas as one who 'went about in this world as a great model of impiety,' then proceeds to describe Judas' torments as an example of the fate of the impious." At that time, impiety meant not pleasing the Greek or Roman gods, nor pleasing society. I'm pretty sure Papias didn't like Judas too much as a person. I could be wrong, though. Needless to say, Judas' life before Jesus was not well documented, and his time described as a disciple was anything but Christ-like. By the sheer fact that he betrayed Jesus, I believe we can all come to the conclusion that he was not a good person, and his life's mark was defined in the moment of handing over the Son of God to be executed.

The Bible provides numerous accounts of Judas—anywhere from mentioning his name to calling him a thief, and giving some details into how he betrayed Jesus. His name is scattered throughout the Gospels (Matthew, Mark, Luke, and John). Of course, as mentioned already, his biggest moment in history was betraying Jesus Christ and handing him over to the Pharisees and government officials at the time to be crucified. So how did he become one of the most negatively crucial pieces of history, and was he chosen by God to do so?

Walking with Jesus through His Struggles

Possible Discrimination

According to the authors at *Bibleinfo,* in the article "Who Were the 12 Disciples," based on his origin, Judas Iscariot may have been different from the other apostles. It has been noted throughout the scripture and historical records that all of the disciples were from Galilee, but Judas was from Judah. He was different from the other disciples. His past made him different; it may have made him the outcast. Have you ever been different from someone else? Of course you have. Is this case, Judas was from somewhere the other were not and that made him different. Could this have had something to do with his betraying Jesus? It could have. Is there enough evidence to prove this? No. He may or may not have held on to the fact that he was from Judah and Jesus was from Galilee. He may have had some discriminatory aggression towards Jesus and the rest of the disciples. But then why follow Jesus in the first place? If there was some anger towards Jesus and/or any member(s) of the group, why stick around? Of course, Scripture does not tell us of any discrimination between the disciples, even for or against Judas. It does tell us that they competed with one another. For example, the disciples discussed who was the greatest in Jesus' eyes. There is not enough hard evidence to conclude that Judas was discriminated against, but in this world when a person is from a different culture then the rest of a group they belong to, often times, they are not accepted like everyone else in the group, no matter how hard they try.

Love of Money

The Bible tells us Judas was the "holder of the purse" for Jesus and his disciples. In John 12:4-6 (NIV), the scripture mentions, *"⁴ But one of his disciples, Judas Iscariot, who was later to betray him, objected, ⁵ 'Why wasn't this perfume sold and the money given to the poor? It was worth a year's wages.' ⁶ He did not say this because he cared about the poor but because he was a thief; as keeper of the money bag, he used to help himself to what was put into it."*

I believe John mentions this in his gospel to show the true mindset of Judas. Of course, John wrote his gospel after Jesus had been crucified, so there may have been just a tad bit of tension or pure hatred against Judas, but nonetheless, he mentions this instance with purpose. By this statement, we find out that Judas, if you didn't take it away from the whole "taking money to kill Jesus" thing, loved money. I believe money was one of his downfalls. The love of money was not the only issue Judas struggled with.

Pride

There are many theories out there on why Judas Iscariot betrayed Jesus. Whichever one you choose to believe, all I ask is that you do your homework before jumping to conclusions. At the end of the day, all we need to remember about Judas is that he betrayed the Son of Man and is paying the price for it. I believe this has interested folks for a couple of thousand years since the betrayal occurred. The hard part of fully understanding the story is that we, as readers of the Bible and other texts from that period, get bits and pieces. We only have part of the story. Even non-biblical text from the B.C.–A.D. century mark can't agree on what truly happened.

Most of the texts about Judas, which are not "biblical" per se, but are based on biblical statements, begin with him "being destined" or "being foreordained" to betray Jesus. I would agree. Jesus gives us that in John 6:70 (NIV): *"Jesus told His disciples, 'Have I not chosen you, the Twelve? Yet one of you is a devil!'"*

Next, the non-biblical texts discuss something along the lines of him being a thief and a patriot to the Roman Empire. Then, the story may read something of jealousy and greed. These all may or may not be the case. I'm not sure there is enough fact to back any of these historical (or non-historical) references up, except those that align with what we read in the scripture of the Bible. I will give you one more thought that I have not seen discussed. Pride.

It was God's will for one of the disciples to betray Jesus. The first we hear about it in the Bible is in Matthew 26:14–16 (NIV):

"14 Then one of the Twelve—the one called Judas Iscariot—went to the chief priests 15 and asked, 'What are you willing to give me if I deliver him over to you?' So they counted out for him thirty pieces of silver. 16 From then on Judas watched for an opportunity to hand him over."

Then, at what is referred to as "The Last Supper," the Bible tells us in verses 20–21 (NIV), *"20 When evening came, Jesus was reclining at the table with the Twelve. 21 And while they were eating, he said, 'Truly I tell you, one of you will betray me.'"*

Similar verses are given to us in Mark 14:10–11, 17–18; Luke 22:1–6, 21–22; John 13:2, 21. All four gospels touch on this piece of information. Each author tells the story a little bit differently and focuses on slightly different items of interest, which is likely due to the personality of the author. None of the scripture really touches on Judas' character, except for being a thief and being destined to betray Jesus. This aspect of Judas' destiny has confused a lot of people over the centuries. People need something to relate to. Do they want to be related to Judas in any way? No, most likely not. Let me ask you the question, would you want to be remembered by all generations to come as the one who betrayed this world's one true savior? Probably not.

Logically, betraying someone you walk with and are friends with for years is not an easy thing to do. It takes a lot of preemptive thought, and most people don't have the evil desire to do so. Sin (and the Devil) have a weird way of getting to people's hearts and minds. To me, in my life, it has always been my pride that tears me down. I know I am not alone in that matter. My first inkling in everything I do is, "I got this." The "I" is probably the largest "I" you can ever imagine. In being human, and knowing many humans for a long time now (34 years to be more precise), I can honestly tell you that our pride typically gets in the way of what God has planned for our lives. I submit to you that it is the root cause for most, if not all, of our failures. I'm just another author, with another thought and another way of looking at the horse that has been beaten to death, but maybe Judas' pride was his fall. In the scriptures, Jesus only ever names Judas by name at the Last Supper. The Bible tells us that Satan entered Judas to fulfill the task of betraying Jesus. Was Satan in Judas his entire life, or may it have been at some point near or at the Last Supper that Satan entered Judas? Up until that point, it may only have been his pride driving him. Think of how you are in your own life. When you sin (and we all do), is it your intent to sin, or does it come naturally? A lot of people, Christians and non-Christians alike, try to diminish sin and practice self-control from the sinful things of this world.

Truly, sometimes it takes supernatural strength—which as humans we do not possess—to overcome the temptations of this world and our own evil desire to sin. Otherwise, we trust in ourselves to be able to accomplish whatever life throws our way. We do not possess the power to overcome Satan on our own. We need a savior. Not truly walking with Jesus (even though he physically did) could have been the cause of Judas' pride getting in the way of being a true disciple of Jesus and living in accordance with God's will.

Brokenness

Besides the love of money and pride, I believe Judas was flat out broken. Judas is a character that so many people can relate too. They don't want to relate to him because he has the worst résumé in the history of mankind. No one wants that title. He didn't even want that title; that's why he killed himself. Every person on this earth, in some way, shape, or form, is broken. The fall of mankind in Genesis was the first time man was broken. When Adam and Eve sinned, mankind was doomed. God allowed man to be broken. God allowed Adam and Eve the opportunity to go against His will for their lives. God allowed for brokenness in the world, and He still does to this very day and will continue to allow it in the future. Why?

God allows us to be broken because, then and only then, do we have the choice to be broken. God could have made us all perfect; plain and simple, our all-powerful God could have done this. But here we are—we are broken.

Imagine a world where everyone is perfect. It would be Heaven on Earth. What would be the need for Heaven? Would there be a need for God? If everyone was perfect, they would not need to cry out to God or love God, because they would be a god. Why would God create a bunch of gods that would not love Him? So instead, He created us, ones who were destined to fail—ones who would be broken. I wholeheartedly believe that He wants us to strive for perfection, to live in His love, and prosper in His grace forever. But brokenness is often followed by failing. In life, when we are in the most pain and in the deepest depths of our existence, this is when we turn to stupid things. We all make stupid choices. Some are more stupid than others. I used the term "stupid" out of love in this context. In our brokenness is where pain and misery accompany us the most. Satan is very good at trying to make us feel comfortable in our misery and in our brokenness.

Take Judas for instance. The writers of the New Testament make Judas out to be a crooked, sorry type of man. He was most likely already this type of person before becoming a disciple, but we cannot be sure. Maybe the Pharisees saw his weakness (money) and saw their opportunity to take Jesus out (or so they thought). Regardless, Satan got to Judas; enough so to betray the Son of God. Judas was a disciple of Jesus Christ, and the lowest point of his life was a lack of competence in that role. Before his discipleship, based on his assumed background and upbringing, we can only ascertain that he probably wasn't the best choice for a disciple. But Jesus chose "rag-tag" types of people as His disciples for His purpose. And let's face it, there had to be one who would betray Jesus to fulfill the Old Testament scriptures of the savior God would send for His people; a sacrificial lamb to wipe away the sins of the world. Someone had to be the one who would be broken enough to think that betraying Jesus was a great idea. Of course, he was willed by Satan, so we can cut him a little slack. But if this did not occur, the whole world (and all future generations) would not have the opportunity to so easily be saved by the blood and resurrection of Jesus Christ.

Could God have found another way to save the people of this world other than them making animal and food sacrifices for the rest of existence on this earth? Of course. Did God need Judas to betray Jesus to allow for people to have an easier way to find Him as their lord and savior? No. But God chose this to be His will for all of humanity. Could he have allowed someone else to betray Jesus? Absolutely. Though God is all-powerful, He has given us free will to choose whom we follow. God did not make Judas betray Jesus—Judas chose that path out of selfish ambition. God uses every deed on this earth for His plan and the purpose He has for all of us. This is how brilliant God is—He can take the most evil of people and use them to change the course of history for the good of mankind and for His kingdom.

Method of betrayal (a kiss)

In Matthew 26:21, the disciple Matthew tells us that Jesus knew one of his disciples would betray him. He states, *"Truly, I say to you, one of you will betray me."* I know myself well enough that if I knew someone was going to kill me, I would at the least try to stop them. If it meant giving all of mankind a chance to be saved, I might reconsider, but I would definitely not react like Jesus did and continue to have a meal with the guy. I would at least walk over and punch the guy in the face. You know, at least inflict some sort of physical pain before he offed me. But of course, Jesus is who he is, and I am who I am. We'll just say that striving to be like him is something I'm working on.

The Bible is like a movie in some cases; there are certain things that happen, and it seems that when it is being read, there should be that creepy background music. Matthew 26:21 was one of those moments captured in the Bible that's similar to the climax of a good action film, like when the main character kills all the bad guys, and he or she walks into the last room to defuse the bomb, then the last bad guy, who is the toughest, is still standing in his or her way. For you sports fans, it's like when the underdog is about to take down the best team in the league, for the championship, and is down by a point with three seconds left on the clock. The only difference is that movies and sporting event outcomes are not an action which determines the fate of all mankind.

The Bible gives multiple accounts of Judas giving Jesus a kiss on the cheek to identify to the soldiers who he was. This one action told the soldiers who to arrest. These accounts are Matthew 26:49, Luke 22:48, and Mark 14:45. That kiss was the moment of betrayal that not only affected the people of that time but every single person who would dwell on this earth and in Heaven, post the resurrection of Jesus Christ. That moment is where the Bible's plot thickens; it is the Bible's climax, if you will. That kiss impacted every soul for the rest of eternity. I submit to you that we should look at it in a different light. If this betrayal wouldn't have happened, we may all have been destined for Hell. Or, we would still be making sacrifices for our sins, as people did in the Old Testament. The kiss defined Jesus, in that very moment, as a criminal who needed to be escorted away by armed soldiers and punished for a crime. Unbeknownst to Judas, it defined Jesus as the one true sacrifice for the sins of the world. For those without hope, He gave them hope, and for those without love, He was love. One of the most evil men of all time betrayed the Son of Man with one of the most loving symbols. He could have simply pointed at Jesus and said, "Hey, that's the guy." But instead, Judas may have been conflicted. He may have been so twisted that he thought he was betraying Jesus out of love. He may have just been crazy. We'll never know why a kiss, but we do know this one kiss changed the world.

Throughout the ages, Judas' kiss has become known as an international sign of betrayal. It is known by the Christian culture as the moment in which Jesus Christ, the Son of God, was betrayed. In the United States of America (it may be in other parts of the world as well), there is a saying: "Don't be a Judas." It's right up there with another saying I have heard occasionally throughout my life: "Don't be a Benedict Arnold." According to the *Encyclopedia Britannica*, Benedict Arnold was similar to Judas in such a way that he was loyal to the colonists' cause during the American Revolutionary War. By the way he was treated by his leadership, he became a traitor in favor of the British Forces. The "don't be" statements refer to someone in a seat of power, those very close to the leadership of a movement that changes the course of history, and for some reason or another, they jump sides at the last minute, ending up on the wrong side of history. As I ponder that thought, the mystery in my mind that remains is what it feels like to betray leadership in such a way that you give up your whole life for a little bit of money or gain. Furthermore, in Judas' case, how would it feel to hand over the Son of God to be killed? I mean, literally, physically, send Him to His death? Not just any quick death, but a brutally slow and unbearably painful death.

Imagine with me for a minute, someone you care about. It could be your mom, your dad, your son, your daughter, sister, brother, friend, etc. Think as if they had not committed any crime, nor had done anything to harm you or anyone else you care about. Imagine they are blameless, even though it is impossible for any human to be purely blameless (except Jesus). Imagine their heart is pure and that they serve the one true God with all of their mind, heart, and soul. The only people they have offended are those who oppose God and are a sickness to society, yet they still love them anyway. See them performing signs, wonders, and miracles. Envision them healing the sick, the blind, the hungry, the lame, the demon-possessed, the needy, the weary, the downtrodden, and the damned. Hear them pouring out their thoughts of God, and witnessing to everyone they come in contact with. Watch as your friend is swarmed with the attention of the people. They gain the love of the crowd just by walking through any place in front of them.

Now imagine your jealousy of them, watching them heal the wounded and not heal you, even though you walked with them daily for three years. It's sickening. It should have been you that was healed; it should have been you that didn't have to worry or feel the pain of this world, while you basked in the glory of the people. Feel the hatred burning inside of you from your broken heart of not having your desires met. Know that your friend loves those people in the crowd more than the others that walked with you for those three years. They are more important to Christ than you are. You know they play favorites. Their favorite disciple is probably John, or maybe Peter, or could it even be Matthew, Mark, or Luke? Yeah, your friend hangs out with John quite a bit. John has their ear; whatever John recommended, I'm pretty sure they listened.

Imagine Satan has entered you, and God allowed it, and you are ready to pounce on the chance to redeem your name, to be above all other names of all the followers. The opportunity arises, and you are paid 30 pieces of silver to hand your friend over to the authorities on false charges that you were promised would stick. Now imagine you go to a garden where your friend is praying, you kiss him or her on the cheek; you have turned your friend over to the authorities to die a slow, painful, and agonizing death—the same friend that loved you in any circumstance, even when they knew you were stealing from them and plotting to have them killed behind their back. You have turned your friend over to people who will beat, torture, and kill them by putting them on a cross to bleed out from all their wounds. How do you feel?

His Death

Judas' death is no mystery. He was so ingrained with the guilt of handing Jesus over to the authorities that he hanged himself. Makes sense. If you turned over the Son of God, your friend that you had followed around for three or so years, to be executed, you would feel pretty terrible too. Regardless of what happened to Judas, God's will was done. It continued to be done even after Judas was dead. Prophecies were fulfilled. Like Judas' life, should we be too concerned with the details not given to us in the scripture? Probably not.

Matthew 27: 3–10 (NIV) gives the explanation of Judas' death by saying, *"³ When Judas, who had betrayed him, saw that Jesus was condemned, he was seized with remorse and returned the thirty pieces of silver to the chief priests and the elders. ⁴ 'I have sinned,' he said, 'for I have betrayed innocent blood.' 'What is that to us?' they replied. 'That's your responsibility.' ⁵ So Judas threw the money into the temple and left. Then he went away and hanged himself. ⁶ The chief priests picked up the coins and said, 'It is against the law to put this into the treasury, since it is blood money.' ⁷ So they decided to use the money to buy the potter's field as a burial place for foreigners. ⁸ That is why it has been called the Field of Blood to this day. ⁹ Then what was spoken by Jeremiah the prophet was fulfilled: 'They took the thirty pieces of silver, the price set on him by the people of Israel, ¹⁰ and they used them to buy the potter's field, as the Lord commanded me.'"*

In Matthew 27:9–10, the Bible tells us what happens to the money Judas took from the Chief Priests to hand over Jesus to them. The amount was 30 pieces of silver, and the Chief Priests would not put the money back in their treasury. Instead, they commanded that it be used to buy a Potter's Field, and the writer, Matthew, points out that these actions were prophesied by the Prophet Jeremiah. Moreover, in Zechariah 11:12–13, the Bible tells us of how Jeremiah contested internally with God about how Israel was treating him. I believe this to be the reference that Matthew 10 specifically refers to when saying that the 30 pieces of silver were used to buy the Potter's field. At this point in Jeremiah's story, he had realized that Israel hated him, and he really didn't want to lead them as a prophet any longer. In verses 7–9 (NIV), he explains, "*7 So I shepherded the flock marked for slaughter, particularly the oppressed of the flock. Then I took two staffs and called one Favor and the other Union, and I shepherded the flock. 8 In one month I got rid of the three shepherds. The flock detested me, and I grew weary of them 9 and said, 'I will not be your shepherd. Let the dying die, and the perishing perish. Let those who are left eat one another's flesh.'"*

As he is saying this in frustration, he continues in verses 12 and 13 (and here is the kicker), "*12 I told them, 'If you think it best, give me my pay; but if not, keep it.' So they paid me thirty pieces of silver. 13 And the Lord said to me, 'Throw it to the potter'—the handsome price at which they valued me! So I took the thirty pieces of silver and threw them to the potter at the house of the Lord.*"

Just as the 30 pieces of silver Judas was given to betray Jesus, Jeremiah was given 30 pieces of silver he received from the people of the time. This was how much the people of the time thought he was worth for being their shepherd (their prophet). This money was also "thrown to the potter." The Bible does not tell us whether or not it was to buy a field, but it was given to the potter nonetheless. In both cases, money (30 pieces of silver) is given to a potter. In both cases, the money is given to the potter because of a series of events that stemmed from a great betrayal. In both cases, the persons committing the betrayal were excused from the presence of God and (as far as we know) were never permitted to be in good graces with God again. One difference that may be pondered from the passage in Matthew was the 30 pieces of silver was commanded to be spent on the potter's field for a burial ground for the local population, and the command was given by the Chief Priests (a.k.a. the bad guys of the story). In Jeremiah's case, God commanded him to give the money to the potter. In this instance, God commanded it, so the prophecy may be set in motion. With the Chief Priests ordering the purchase in Matthew 10, this shows that even when sinful acts occur, God still has control of the situation. God allowed the prophecy to be fulfilled.

Continuing down the path of Jeremiah's prophecy, in Jeremiah 32, he wrote of a time when he was consulted by God to purchase a field from his cousin, Hanamel. In those days, the scripture tells us, in order to purchase the land, Jeremiah had to have rights to the land. Verse 7 tells us that Jeremiah was the "nearest relative," so it was his right and duty to buy it. Let's stop there for a second. If someone came to you and said, "Hey, you have to buy your uncle's land because you're the nearest relative," would you just buy it? Personally, I'd probably be like, "I'll take the land, but I would prefer not to pay for it." Maybe I'm just cheap, but land, even in those days, was pretty pricey. Anyway, Jeremiah felt a calling from God to buy the land, so he had a pretty good reason for buying it. If given the same situation, I would probably buy it as well.

Further, in Jeremiah 18:1–10 (NIV), the Bible tells of a message Jeremiah receives from God. It reads, *"¹ This is the word that came to Jeremiah from the Lord: ² 'Go down to the potter's house, and there I will give you my message.' ³ So I went down to the potter's house, and I saw him working at the wheel. ⁴ But the pot he was shaping from the clay was marred in his hands; so the potter formed it into another pot, shaping it as seemed best to him. ⁵ Then the word of the Lord came to me. ⁶ He said, 'Can I not do with you, Israel, as this potter does?' declares the Lord. 'Like clay in the hand of the potter, so are you in my hand, Israel. ⁷ If at any time I announce that a nation or kingdom is to be uprooted, torn down and destroyed, ⁸ and if that nation I warned repents of its evil, then I will relent and not inflict on it the disaster I had planned. ⁹ And if at another time I announce that a nation or kingdom is to be built up and planted, ¹⁰ and if it does evil in my sight and does not obey me, then I will reconsider the good I had intended to do for it.'"*

The people of Israel, in the time of Jeremiah, were doing some bad stuff, like worshiping idols. God continued to tell Jeremiah of the disaster He was preparing for the people of Judah if they did not repent and turn from their ways (chapter 18, verse 11).

In verse 12, once Jeremiah tells the people what God had said, the people react by saying, "It's no use. We will continue with our own plans; we will all follow the stubbornness of our evil hearts."

What God said to that was basically (in a nutshell) the people of that nation were going to face His wrath. Word to the wise: don't anger God so much that He brings His wrath upon you. It is never going to work out for you, or most likely your children, and/or their children (if you have children, that is). The people of Israel, in this case, made a poor choice on how to treat God and Jeremiah. They later plot against Jeremiah. Needless to say, I'm not sure they won the fight with God. This passage reminds us of a time when God condemned Israel for their actions. Also, God compares Himself to a potter, by instituting that He controls Israel's destiny, like a potter molding clay in His hands. Simply put, this is one reference to the prophecy of Judas betraying Jesus and using the money to buy a field and interacting with a potter to fulfill God's plan.

The Field of Blood: Before Mathias was chosen to replace Judas, the Bible tells us that Peter spells out the end of Judas' life in Acts 1:15–20 (NIV). The scripture reads, *"[15] In those days Peter stood up among the believers (a group numbering about a hundred and twenty) [16] and said, 'Brothers and sisters, the Scripture had to be fulfilled in which the Holy Spirit spoke long ago through David concerning Judas, who served as guide for those who arrested Jesus. [17] He was one of our number and shared in our ministry.' [18] (With the payment he received for his wickedness, Judas bought a field; there he fell headlong, his body burst open and all his intestines spilled out. [19] Everyone in Jerusalem heard about this, so they called that field in their language Akeldama, that is, Field of Blood.) [20] 'For,' said Peter, 'it is written in the Book of Psalms: "May his place be deserted; let there be no one to dwell in it," and, "May another take his place of leadership."'*"

Let me tell you, if when you die, and the place you pass away in is called the "Field of Blood," and no one will dwell in it, (the local government uses it to bury the dead of "foreigners" or during that time, people they didn't like) you know you have done something wrong with your life. Regardless of being destined to do something or doing by choice, you have just done something wrong. On the other hand, the bar is set pretty low on being a bad person in life. If the whole "field" thing doesn't happen for you, good work, you weren't as disgusting as Judas was. God has given us the ability to have free will. Judas took the steps to betray Jesus; as such, the field he killed himself in will be forever known as the "Field of Blood." You and I, as well as every other human being on this planet, have free will. Let's all try to use it wisely so we don't wind up with our burial place being called the "Field of Blood".

3

THE PATHS

The *Merriam-Webster Dictionary* defines the term "free will" as a noun that means "voluntary choice or decision." Another way it is defined is, "freedom of humans to make choices that are not determined by prior causes or by divine intervention." In these two definitions specifically, we see the word "choice(s)." Without choice, one has no free will. Without choice, there is no consequence. Without consequence, there is no plan. Without a plan, there is no will. Without will there is no purpose. And without purpose, there is no reason for existence. Simply put, free will is thought put into action. It is using judgment to exercise a will. Will comes from the little voice inside of you that tells you what to do. Any common–day psychologist will tell you it's your "psyche," commonly known to "normal" people as your soul spirit, or conscience.

As the Bible tells us, God made man in His own image (Genesis 1:27). Every man, woman, and child has a spirit living inside of them. We know this because the Bible explains this concept on numerous accounts. Here are some examples:

Genesis 3:19 (NIV) *"By the sweat of your brow you will eat your food until you return to the ground, since from it you were taken; for dust you are and to dust you will return."*

Psalm 146:4 (NIV) *"When their spirit departs, they return to the ground; on that very day their plans come to nothing."*

Ecclesiastes 12:7 (NIV) *"...and the dust returns to the ground it came from, and the spirit returns to God who gave it."*

So we know that one's soul or spirit, and also intellect, gives a person the ability to make decisions freely. For instance, the laws we follow in our society are based on people exercising free will, in either obeying or disobeying the law. If someone decides to abide by the laws of God or of the land, there will be no negative consequence, but if someone decides to break the law, there are consequences he or she must deal with.

In Romans 7 and 8, Paul writes about our sinful nature. Yes, I believe we are born of a sinful nature. (Oh no, the nature versus nurture discussion!) So, I'm not going to go into that discussion exactly. I'll touch on it only because Paul defines his sinful nature and how he handles it within the text of his books. In verses 14–25 of Chapter 7 of the book of Romans (NIV), Paul explains the sinful nature he was born with—that we were all born with.

"¹⁴ We know that the law is spiritual; but I am unspiritual, sold as a slave to sin. ¹⁵ I do not understand what I do. For what I want to do I do not do, but what I hate I do. ¹⁶ And if I do what I do not want to do, I agree that the law is good. ¹⁷ As it is, it is no longer I myself who do it, but it is sin living in me. ¹⁸ For I know that good itself does not dwell in me, that is, in my sinful nature. For I have the desire to do what is good, but I cannot carry it out. ¹⁹ For I do not do the good I want to do, but the evil I do not want to do—this I keep on doing. ²⁰ Now if I do what I do not want to do, it is no longer I who do it, but it is sin living in me that does it. ²¹ So I find this law at work: Although I want to do good, evil is right there with me. ²² For in my inner being I delight in God's law; ²³ but I see another law at work in me, waging war against the law of my mind and making me a prisoner of the law of sin at work within me. ²⁴ What a wretched man I am! Who will rescue me from this body that is subject to death? ²⁵ Thanks be to God, who delivers me through Jesus Christ our Lord! So then, I myself in my mind am a slave to God's law, but in my sinful nature a slave to the law of sin."

From a simplistic sense, if only looking at this passage, there are two things that drive people's destiny: good and evil. Good tendencies create opportunities and evil tendencies create obstacles in our lives. But God being the God that He is uses both for the benefits of His plan. For His chosen, He uses both good and evil for their benefit; in return His chosen give glory and honor to Him.

In Romans 7, Paul speaks as if he has no choice in the matter of doing evil. That even when he tries to do good, evil always finds a way to creep in. In Romans 8, he clears things up on the matter of choice. In verses 9–11 (NIV), *"⁹ You, however, are not in the realm of the flesh but are in the realm of the Spirit, if indeed the Spirit of God lives in you. And if anyone does not have the Spirit of Christ, they do not belong to Christ. ¹⁰ But if Christ is in you, then even though your body is subject to death because of sin, the Spirit gives life because of righteousness. ¹¹ And if the Spirit of him who raised Jesus from the dead is living in you, he who raised Christ from the dead will also give life to your mortal bodies because of his Spirit who lives in you."*

In a nutshell, he states we have a choice to choose the Spirit over the flesh and vice versa. I submit to you that God allows us to fail, just as he allows us to succeed. Failure, like success, is how we learn and grow as humans. In some cases, we learn more by failing than by succeeding. In this passage, Paul is really talking about your flesh causing you to fail. "How does that relate to being predestined?" you may ask. First, let's look at the term "predestine" and what it truly means. Again, using The Merriam-Webster *Dictionary*, to be "predestined" is to be "destined, decreed, determined, appointed, or settled beforehand". And the term "destiny" has a couple of definitions:

"Something to which a person or thing is destined: fortune."

"A predetermined course of events often held to be an irresistible power or agency."

Based on the definitions of being predestined and the term "destiny," and what we know by Romans 7, we can take away that we are predestined to sin by our own flesh and desires. The difference these verses call out is how we deal with our sin. We can either be in Christ or not; either way, we have to deal with our sin. Destiny is simply an inevitable choice we make or are going to make, followed by the outcome of that choice. It's putting one's free will into action. It sends us down one path or another.

Have you ever thought to yourself, *Do the choices I make affect those around me? How am I affected by my choices?* If you do not openly admit to thinking these things before, you are most likely blocking out your own thoughts. Mentally, you're not all there, or you are lying to yourself. If one is legally sane, then most likely everyone has pondered these questions, or ones like them at some point. It's a part of human nature to care what others think about us. It's also human nature to think of one's own self all of the time. So the question should not be, "Do the choices I make affect those around me?" It should be, "How do I make better choices to positively impact those around me?" Proverbs 4 (NIV) has that answer:

> *1 Listen, my sons, to a father's instruction;*
> *pay attention and gain understanding.*
> *2 I give you sound learning,*
> *so do not forsake my teaching.*
> *3 For I too was a son to my father,*
> *still tender, and cherished by my mother.*
> *4 Then he taught me, and he said to me,*
> *"Take hold of my words with all your heart;*
> *keep my commands, and you will live.*
> *5 Get wisdom, get understanding;*
> *do not forget my words or turn away from them.*
> *6 Do not forsake wisdom, and she will protect you;*
> *love her, and she will watch over you.*
> *7 The beginning of wisdom is this: Get[a] wisdom.*
> *Though it cost all you have,[b] get understanding.*
> *8 Cherish her, and she will exalt you;*
> *embrace her, and she will honor you.*
> *9 She will give you a garland to grace your head*
> *and present you with a glorious crown."*
>
> *10 Listen, my son, accept what I say,*
> *and the years of your life will be many.*

JORDAN M. RIEDEL

*¹¹ I instruct you in the way of wisdom
    and lead you along straight paths.
¹² When you walk, your steps will not be hampered;
    when you run, you will not stumble.
¹³ Hold on to instruction, do not let it go;
    guard it well, for it is your life.
¹⁴ Do not set foot on the path of the wicked
    or walk in the way of evildoers.
¹⁵ Avoid it, do not travel on it;
    turn from it and go on your way.
¹⁶ For they cannot rest until they do evil;
    they are robbed of sleep till they make someone stumble.
¹⁷ They eat the bread of wickedness
    and drink the wine of violence.*

*¹⁸ The path of the righteous is like the morning sun,
    shining ever brighter till the full light of day.
¹⁹ But the way of the wicked is like deep darkness;
    they do not know what makes them stumble.*

*²⁰ My son, pay attention to what I say;
    turn your ear to my words.
²¹ Do not let them out of your sight,
    keep them within your heart;
²² for they are life to those who find them
    and health to one's whole body.
²³ Above all else, guard your heart,
    for everything you do flows from it.
²⁴ Keep your mouth free of perversity;
    keep corrupt talk far from your lips.
²⁵ Let your eyes look straight ahead;
    fix your gaze directly before you.
²⁶ Give careful thought to the[c] paths for your feet
    and be steadfast in all your ways.
²⁷ Do not turn to the right or the left;
    keep your foot from evil.*

CHOSEN

Proverbs 4 tells us that we must keep God's word in our lives and surround our thoughts, our actions, and our deepest affections focused on God. It gives us a few lines on how our world may turn if we follow evil and/or those who do evil things. Verses 20–27 capture how we should protect ourselves from the evil of this world. By protecting ourselves from evil, we make our paths align with God's will. As God often does, he gives us many ways to look at things, so we can gain wisdom and understanding. And as Proverbs 4 alludes to, we should give everything to gain wisdom and understanding.

Bear with me on this, and try to think of life as a Sudoku puzzle. Traditional Sudoku is a game by which there is a nine-box by nine-box square. Within the nine-box by nine-box square, there are nine three-box by three-box boxes that fit the numbers one through nine in them. The goal of the game is to put the numbers (one through nine) in each column and row and to also have one through nine in each of the nine three-box by three-box squares. In Sudoku, the player is given some of the individual boxes filled in with a random set of numbers. Depending on what level your puzzle is at, it could be many, or it could be few. Nonetheless, there is always a beginning, middle, and end to the puzzle.

In the beginning, when first thinking of what numbers to look for, one can always point out the obvious solutions. Once all of the obvious solutions have been unraveled (depending on the level of difficulty of the puzzle and a person's intellectual capacity to solve puzzles of this nature), the player must continuously look for patterns of numbers to find more solutions. The end of the puzzle could mean one of two things. First, the player could have completed the puzzle. The other may mean the player gave up on completing the puzzle and went and did something else with their time.

Say you are trying to complete a Sudoku puzzle of your life. You had a beginning (birth), you have a middle (which you are in, as part of your current state), and you will have an end to your life (a.k.a. death and your final purpose). Sudoku serves as a means for entertainment and, for some folks, intellectual stimulation and/or a form of learning. It could even be a purpose of life for some folks. Who am I to judge? To me, I find it to be entertaining and something to pass the time with. Also, it makes me tired when my mind won't stop being restless from the day's events. Regardless, for this example, it serves as a way to look at life and purpose, and will hopefully help us examine ourselves.

When you're figuring out this Sudoku puzzle of life, there are maneuvers that are going to be more transparent than others, and some that you will have to work a little harder to figure out. If you are trying to solve an extremely difficult puzzle, you will have to look five to ten moves ahead to even solve it; you have to implement memorization into the equation. Simply put, in life, there are hard things and easy things, and they are at all levels of difficulty. Some folks take a little bit longer to figure out the puzzle than others. Sometimes folks find their purpose and life (complete the puzzle), and others miss the boat (give up on trying to solve the puzzle). But if everyone would sit down long enough and have the desire to finish the puzzle, they would eventually figure it out—by themselves or with the help of others' guidance. It may take the help of others to find your purpose in life. In Sudoku, there is always a solution to the puzzle. Every person in this life has a purpose. Sometimes, we may lose sight of our purpose, our solution to life's puzzle. Ultimately, the reason for our existence and a key to help you find your solution to life's challenges is to believe in the following things: loving others, loving God, believing Jesus Christ died for the sins of the world, fearing God, and keeping His commandments.

In the case of missing one's purpose, try picturing life like the card game Solitaire. It is a game one plays alone, like living one's own life. Like Sudoku, it may or may not be a game someone may play when they want to feel alone or try to control every move they make. I'm sure there is a story or history lesson of when Solitaire came about, and how it came to be on every home PC, installed and ready to play, with no need to download anything or purchase any additional software. Solitaire is at the user's fingertips from the day they purchase their computer. Does it sound like the desires of our generation so far?

Say you started playing a game of Solitaire. The first step you may take is to see what cards pop up that show you their face value, the initial flip. You may or may not be able to make a move or two or three. Sometimes, you may be able to make ten or more moves depending on what cards pop up on the initial flip and which cards lie underneath them. In some cases, though, there are two cards of the same value. In other circumstances, the player may only have the ability to move one of the two cards with equal value, but not both. Herein comes a choice that may or may not change the outcome of the game, depending on what the player chooses. Sometimes in life, we come to a crossroads and we can either go right, or we can go left. If my life, I've come to the conclusion that one rarely is faced with two choices—typically it is more. This is where one needs God's guidance to find His purpose for their life.

Such as in Solitaire, we may be faced with four of the same valued cards if we chose to move one card versus another of the same value, onto the card of the opposite color and a value of one greater, different outcomes. In solitaire, such as in life, we face multiple outcomes from many different valued cards. The end goal is to win the game. Every human being has an idea in their own mind of what success looks like. They have an end goal to just about everything they face. They have ideas of what they want their life to look like at certain stages and even possibly what their death looks like. The Bible discussed such choice-making in Proverbs:

Proverbs 14:12 (NKJV) *"There is a way that seems right to a man, but in the end leads to death."*

This verse is a warning to mankind. God is telling us to not make choices on our own understanding, but to trust in Him and to trust what He says in His word. Solitaire is a game of chance and luck. Due to the player having to guess in some circumstances, the game of Solitaire may not allow the player to win the game every time. Sudoku is a puzzle and does allow for a solution every single time, as long as the player does not make any mistakes. No matter how many choices one may make during a single game or puzzle, it may not lead to victory or completion. In life, as in the games of Solitaire and Sudoku, we can only see what cards are facing up and what numbers are displayed in front of us. God can see everything else. Walking by faith in God is a true art. In my life, I have discovered this to be both the easy way and most difficult way. I prefer the easy way whenever possible, but sometimes God allows us to make stupid choices, so we may grow from our mistakes. Sometimes the hard way is the only way. In Solitaire, the cards we are dealt will never be the cards we could have guessed, likewise in Sudoku, each puzzle brings new numbers in new boxes, which brings a new challenge. They will never be the cards or numbers we want to see all the time. The only way to receive the cards or numbers that you want is to align your games and puzzles with God's will. He may not give you everything you want, but if you love Him, He will give you everything He knows is best for you. Then, cards and numbers don't matter anymore, and they are no longer have a hold on your life. Surrendering yourself to God is the best thing you will ever do in this life. It's not easy, because our flesh will always crave something of this world, but God is all-powerful, and He will see you through.

We are all born into a sinful nature. We are all born imperfect; this makes us all equal. Taking out the money and resources aspect of it, the richest person in the world has the same problems with flesh and bones as the poorest person in the world. We all face the choice to sin. But if we set our eyes upon Jesus, and He will deliver us from Satan's ultimate strategy to win: death.

How are we like Judas? (Sinful nature)

I would first like to get something off my chest. I am a sinner. You are a sinner. We are all sinners. I take you back to Romans 3:23, where the Bible tells us *"we all have sinned and fallen short of the Glory of God."* Every one of us has a collection of sin we have committed, and as long as we are on Earth, we will continue to live with a sinful nature. As human beings, we face and will continue to face trials and tribulations of many types. God has never promised us that being human would be easy. He has never promised that our "Christian" walk would be a glorified walk in the park. We will never be perfect. In all actuality, we deserve death. For all the sins we have committed and will commit, we deserve to be put to death.

This may come as a bit of a surprise to some of you. I'm going to say this in a quiet voice, so as not to make it awkward for you: "Judas was a sinner too." I challenge you in this part of this message to try to relate to Judas. In what we know about him, he was one of Jesus' disciples. He walked with Him for a good three years or so. He was the one who held the money for the group. Satan entered Judas, as described in Luke 22:3, closely before chatting to the Chief Priests and Elders about betraying Jesus. And in John 13:2, the Bible tells us he was prompted to betray Jesus by Satan. Let's not forget this one: he betrayed Jesus. He was remorseful about betraying Jesus (he tried to give the 30 pieces of silver back to the chief priests and elders). He hanged himself and was replaced as one of the twelve disciples.

Let me ask you now, have you ever done one of the things listed in the previous paragraph? Not all of these things make you a sinner if you have done them; for example, holding money for a group. Obviously, not a sin. Judas was not holding on to the disciples' money with honesty. John 12:6 (ESV) tells us this about Judas: *"He said this, not because he cared about the poor, but because he was a thief, and having charge of the moneybag he used to help himself to what was put into it."* So he was ripping people off. Have you ever abused your authoritative position for personal gain? I'll ask you something that may be a little close to home for some of you. Have you ever tried to manipulate a situation for personal gain? Because you "knew" you were right in the situation? So much so that it caused you to sin to get your way? I know I have. It's very easy for us to do as human beings, even without Satan entering into us.

Take, for instance, an infant. The most innocent human being is an infant that has just come out of the womb and into the world. By the end of their first day of being in this world, they know how to get what they need. In their case, they cry, most of the time it's for a good reason. They're either hungry, have a soiled diaper, are hot or cold, or they just want attention. They cry because they cannot talk. So, we can cut them a little bit of slack. Needless to say, I would say they are 99% of the time just surviving. As they grow older, though, they learn the ways of the world. The Bible tells us in Proverbs 22:6 (NIV) "*Start children off on the way they should go, and even when they are old they will not turn from it.*"

Judas did not have a godly upbringing. I don't know for sure if Judas had a rough childhood. What I do know is he was put in some pretty tough decision-making positions. I know in my life, there have been a couple of times I have made some bad decisions, and there have been some times in my life where I have made bad decision after bad decision after bad decision until I realized I was somewhere I didn't want to be in life, and I know that is not where God wanted me to be either.

Let's take a look at Solomon in the Old Testament; the book of Ecclesiastes to be more precise. In the first two chapters of Ecclesiastes, Solomon goes on and on about how everything in life is meaningless ("vanity" in some versions – Chapter 1 vs. 1–11). In chapter three, Solomon touches on timing. He writes (Chapter 3 vs. 1–8, NIV):

> "*1 There is a time for everything,
>   and a season for every activity under the heavens:
> 2 a time to be born and a time to die,
>   a time to plant and a time to uproot,
> 3 a time to kill and a time to heal,
>   a time to tear down and a time to build,
> 4 a time to weep and a time to laugh,
>   a time to mourn and a time to dance,
> 5 a time to scatter stones and a time to gather them,*

> *a time to embrace and a time to refrain from embracing,*
> *⁶ a time to search and a time to give up,*
> *a time to keep and a time to throw away,*
> *⁷ a time to tear and a time to mend,*
> *a time to be silent and a time to speak,*
> *⁸ a time to love and a time to hate,*
> *a time for war and a time for peace."*

Solomon, throughout the entire book of Ecclesiastes, was pondering his life. He makes the statement over and over again that his life was meaningless. He looked back on his life and pointed out the good things he had done, bad things he had done, and things—both good and bad—he had seen others do. Though some of his conclusions are very vulgar, they are all true. In his piece on timing in chapter three, he mentions a few things like killing and hating. His point is that we shouldn't spend too much time worrying so much about life, but we should enjoy it. It is God's wish for us to enjoy life. God will judge us for all we have done when the day comes, but until that day, it is His wish for us to enjoy life and find peace through Him.

Solomon's point in Ecclesiastes 3:1-8 is that there is a time for everything. According to The *Merriam-Webster Dictionary*, the term "time" has 14 definitions. For discussion purposes let's take a look at two:

1. "The measured or measurable period during which an action, process, or condition exists or continues: duration"

2. "A nonspatial continuum that is measured in terms of events which succeed one another from past through present to future"

Simply put, the term "time" is used to describe existence. Time can be described with a plethora of adjectives. Time can make us feel a certain way. We can count time, and we can count *on* time. We have clocks that tell us what the time is. On any given day, at any given moment, we can know what time it is. We can base our whole lives on, or around, time. God teaches us a lot through time. For example, if God's plan is for us to be still and wait for something, God is and will be teaching us patience through that time. And let me tell you from experience, we learn patience whether we want to or not. Ultimately, God inspired Solomon to tell us that time is irrelevant. Time should not drive our lives. Why? Because sometimes time can get us into trouble. To be more precise, what we do with the time we have can also get us into trouble.

Sometimes in life we dig a hole so deep that we can't get out of it. God wants His children to always be on guard with their souls. He wants this for us because we are like sheep (His sheep), and He is our Shepard. Let me tell you—sheep are dumb. Please take no offense if you love sheep. Contrary to popular belief, even after my previous statements, I do like sheep. We can all be honest; they are not the brightest tools in the toolshed. Let me repeat myself: we are like sheep. Sometimes we make dumb choices. Always have a way out of your dumb choices that bring you back to God. God is not in the business of losing sheep; remember, He is a Shepard—our Shepard. We can't always be too concerned with falling off the beaten path, as long as we know God will be there to pull us back on it. He will not let His chosen people stray too far.

If we look back on how Judas lived the portion of life we *do* know of, he was always critical towards the group. On top of being a thief to Jesus and the disciples, he was always looking out for himself. As we read the passages of the disciples' interactions with one another and other figures in the Gospels, we can see that he was kind of the outcast of the group in every circumstance he was listed in. Of course, Matthew, Mark, Luke, and John wrote their gospels after Jesus had descended into heaven, but they always refer to Judas as the one who betrayed Jesus.

1 John 3: 1–3 (ESV) tells us, *"¹ See what kind of love the Father has given to us that we should be called children of God; and so we are. The reason why the world does not know us is that it did not*

know him. ² Beloved, we are God's children now, and what we will be has not yet appeared; but we know that when he appears we shall be like him, because we shall see him as he is. ³ And everyone who thus hopes in him purifies himself as he is pure."

Judas physically knew Jesus, but he did not truly *know* Jesus. He physically followed Jesus for a period of time in his life, but he was not God's child. In 1 John 3:1, Judas would be considered a part of the "world" that did not know God. He knew the human piece of God, which was Jesus Christ, but he did not truly believe that He was God. There must have been something in Judas' life that held him back from truly knowing Jesus. It could have been his pride or his love of money—we will never know for sure. What we do know is that Judas could not let go of that one, or two, or three, or more thing(s) that kept him from the truth and love that was and still is, Jesus Christ.

We all have things we cannot let go of in this world that keep us from truly knowing the full complexity of God's love for us. In my life, anger towards others is that thing that pulls me away from God's will. Throughout my life, I have gotten stuck being angry at people making "sheep-like" decisions. What I mean by that is when certain things have happened to me, like when someone has hurt me emotionally, I hold on to that anger; I get stuck. I get stuck in the hatred I have for that person and to what they have done. It's almost like that anger has a hold on me. One of Satan's most powerful skillsets is causing confusion, and a lot of the time, anger is caused by confusion. Sometimes it's a small act someone has done to me, and sometimes it's a large act. Regardless of the size, it angers me all the same. It could even be that someone hasn't even done something yet, but there may be potential for someone to do something; with a lot of assuming and confusing, anger overwhelms me. I get stuck in the same old rut. Almost every time, it takes an uncountable number of prayers to get me out of those "anger spouts." Sometimes the barrage of struggle seems insurmountable. I have also realized that these are the tests and trials God allows me to face. These trials have taught me how to be a better Christian through building knowledge, patience, self-control, etc., but that doesn't make the challenges any easier. The challenges continue to grow harder and harder as I grow in Christ. The Bible tells us in James 1:13–15 (NIV), *"*[13] *When tempted, no one should say, 'God is tempting me.' For God cannot be tempted by evil, nor does he tempt anyone;* [14] *but each person is tempted when they are dragged away by their own evil desire and enticed.* [15] *Then, after desire has conceived, it gives birth to sin; and sin, when it is full-grown, gives birth to death."*

The Bible tells us that God does get angry. He gets angry at sin and the people who commit sin. According to Frank Hasel, author of the article, *The Wrath of* God, the Bible uses the term "wrath" in reference to God approximately 455 times in the Old Testament and 375 times in the New Testament. God's wrath or anger is always justified by His perfect love and righteousness. Romans 1:18–20 (NIV) provides a picture of how God's anger can be explained: *"*[18] *The wrath of God is being revealed from heaven against all the godlessness and wickedness of people, who suppress the truth by their wickedness,* [19] *since what may be known about God is plain to them, because God has made it plain to them.* [20] *For since the creation of the world God's invisible qualities—his eternal power and divine nature—have been clearly seen, being understood from what has been made, so that people are without excuse."*

The theme of God's anger, throughout the Bible, tends to be the type of anger a parent has for a child when the child is doing something disobedient. Meaning, they know they should be doing the right thing, but choose not to do the right thing. All anger is not a sin. There is a fine line between how anger can cause sin versus actually being sin itself. It takes a lot of self-findings and prayer to determine how one's anger may be looked at by God (the ultimate judge of character). I have dug deep into the depths of my soul to find that my anger is a cause of my sin. It tends to bring forth actions by which are not of God.

Unjustified/uncontrolled/irrational anger is a sin and/or may cause sin. I fully understand that that type of anger is a sin. My evil desire is to dwell in my anger because that aligns with my pride. God does not call us to be angry and bitter. God does not call us to sin or suffer in anger. The Apostle Paul writes in 1 Thessalonians 5:9–11 (NIV), *"⁹ For God did not appoint us to suffer wrath but to receive salvation through our Lord Jesus Christ. ¹⁰ He died for us so that, whether we are awake or asleep, we may live together with him. ¹¹ Therefore encourage one another and build each other up, just as in fact you are doing."*

"The Flesh" is a product of the world and refers to the how the Bible teaches us about worldly desires placed in our lives by Satan. Anger is not loving. Dwelling in sin is not loving. Dwelling in sin is not of God; it is not part of His plan. Will He use it for His glory? Of course. But does He want us to continue down the path of sin? Of course not.

Think of your worst enemy. If you don't have a worst enemy, then think of the person that is giving you the most grief in this current moment. That person may be called to follow Christ. They may be a Christian at the time they hurt you, or they may come to know Christ after they have hurt you. God will forgive them if they ask and believe. He will forgive them whether or not you have forgiven them. Even yet, if the enemy of your life already claims to be a Christian and following Christ, that doesn't always mean they are one. God will be their ultimate judge; all we can do it work on ourselves and try to forgive others of their actions. Sometimes someone else's "sheep-like" action towards us is meant to guide us. What if that path you thought you were supposed to take wasn't God's path, and that person was sent to stop you from taking the wrong path? Can you forgive that person without ever knowing the "why they did what they did?" 1 Thessalonians 5:15 (NIV) tells us, *"Make sure that nobody pays back wrong for wrong, but always strive to do what is good for each other and for everyone else."* Anger is an emotion, which means God will give his followers the strength to overcome it. Learning to let it go and move on is a key attribute in loving God and loving others.

Ephesians 2:1–10 tells us about once being dead but becoming alive through Jesus. It tells about how God shows us mercy and love when we, sinners, do not deserve it. Every person on this earth sins. The only way we become free of sin is through the blood of Jesus Christ. Likewise, our greatest enemies have the same opportunity. If we do not show them the grace and love God has given us, then God will no longer give us the grace we long for when we sin. Ephesians 2:1–10 (ESV) reads:

"*¹ And you were dead in the trespasses and sins ² in which you once walked, following the course of this world, following the prince of the power of the air, the spirit that is now at work in the sons of disobedience—³ among whom we all once lived in the passions of our flesh, carrying out the desires of the body and the mind, and were by nature children of wrath, like the rest of mankind. ⁴ But God, being rich in mercy, because of the great love with which he loved us, ⁵ even when we were dead in our trespasses, made us alive together with Christ—by grace you have been saved—⁶ and raised us up with him and seated us with him in the heavenly places in Christ Jesus, ⁷ so that in the coming ages he might show the immeasurable riches of his grace in kindness toward us in Christ Jesus. ⁸ For by grace you have been saved through faith. And this is not your own doing; it is the gift of God, ⁹ not a result of works, so that no one may boast. ¹⁰ For we are his workmanship, created in Christ Jesus for good works, which God prepared beforehand, that we should walk in them.*"

Unjustified/uncontrolled/irrational anger is a sin and/or may cause sin. Ephesians 4:26–27 (NIV) says, "*²⁶'In your anger do not sin': Do not let the sun go down while you are still angry, ²⁷ and do not give the devil a foothold.*" What another sinner does to you in this world may crush your life; it may crush your dreams; it may crush your hope. Whatever sinners have done to you, whatever they may continue to do, they may be, or one day may become a child of God. They may receive the same gift God has for you and me. If they are performing acts of wrongdoing towards you, that is on them to take up with God. The Bible tells us when someone is doing something to harm us, to turn the other cheek. I want to encourage you to pray and ask God what that truly means in each situation. I know what turning the other cheek means in an obvious sense, but it may mean something different to you in your situation than how others may interpret it. Seek God and ask for his guidance.

All Sin is Equal

Letting go of things that people have done to us is one of the most difficult things we must do in this life. We feel like we are justified in hating others based on things they have done to us. I submit to you that the disciples felt this way towards Judas. Let's be honest: the man betrayed the son of God and all of His followers. At the same time—and please do not take this as praise for the man—he is the reason Jesus was sent to the cross to die for our sins. The motive of his heart was sinful, but God used the outcome of his motives to transform this world and how we interact with God today. The Bible says in James 2:1–13 (ESV) that we must forgive and not judge; we must be merciful:

"[1] My brothers, show no partiality as you hold the faith in our Lord Jesus Christ, the Lord of glory. [2] For if a man wearing a gold ring and fine clothing comes into your assembly, and a poor man in shabby clothing also comes in, [3] and if you pay attention to the one who wears the fine clothing and say, 'You sit here in a good place,' while you say to the poor man, 'You stand over there,' or, 'Sit down at my feet,' [4] have you not then made distinctions among yourselves and become judges with evil thoughts? [5] Listen, my beloved brothers, has not God chosen those who are poor in the world to be rich in faith and heirs of the kingdom, which he has promised to those who love him? [6] But you have dishonored the poor man. Are not the rich the ones who oppress you, and the ones who drag you into court? [7] Are they not the ones who blaspheme the honorable name by which you were called? [8] If you really fulfill the royal law according to the Scripture, 'You shall love your neighbor as yourself,' you are doing well. [9] But if you show partiality, you are committing sin and are convicted by the law as transgressors. [10] For whoever keeps the whole law but fails in one point has become guilty of all of it. [11] For he who said, 'Do not commit adultery,' also said, 'Do not murder.' If you do not commit adultery but do murder, you have become a transgressor of the law. [12] So speak and so act as those who are to be judged under the law of liberty. [13] For judgment is without mercy to one who has shown no mercy. Mercy triumphs over judgment."

If we are not merciful to others when they have wronged us, then we will not be shown mercy on the final day. We will be judged by how we have judged others. I can take from my own life that the thoughts I have about others, in my anger, is not always godlike. My anger is something I struggle with, and I know that. God knows that as well, but I most certainly need forgiveness for my anger and judgment of others. I have always struggled with loving others. Because let's be honest, it's not easy to love others, especially when humans do "sheep-like" things. But God is love; therefore, we must love to be with God, now and for eternity, for He has called us to love everyone.

There has always been something inside of me that amplifies the feeling of anger. I have heard it described as "seeing red." The chemical reaction that takes place inside our body when we feel the emotion of anger can be very intense. I'm not sure why God made us this way, but the science behind the feeling of anger isn't going to keep me up at night. Anger brings on other types of physical reactions. Aside from the reactions (i.e., shaking, flushed cheeks, facial expressions, etc.), one could see there are also internal changes that occur. Without going into a ton of scientific detail, I'm referring to the feeling of warmth washing over your body, one's heart rate increasing, or blacking out for a split second or a period of time while your body processes the feeling (seeing red), and things of that nature.

It's not easy to control anger. For me, at least, God has had to intervene quite a bit. I have been praying for healing in this regard for most of my life and will most likely have to continue to pray for this struggle for the rest of my life. How do we deal with anger? I believe it's a two-step approach. In considering the first step, Psalm 139 (NIV) is a good example of a verse.

> *[1] You have searched me, LORD,*
> *and you know me.*
> *[2] You know when I sit and when I rise;*
> *you perceive my thoughts from afar.*
> *[3] You discern my going out and my lying down;*

CHOSEN

   you are familiar with all my ways.
⁴ *Before a word is on my tongue*
   you, Lord, know it completely.
⁵ *You hem me in behind and before,*
   and you lay your hand upon me.
⁶ *Such knowledge is too wonderful for me,*
   too lofty for me to attain.
⁷ *Where can I go from your Spirit?*
   Where can I flee from your presence?
⁸ *If I go up to the heavens, you are there;*
   if I make my bed in the depths, you are there.
⁹ *If I rise on the wings of the dawn,*
   if I settle on the far side of the sea,
¹⁰ *even there your hand will guide me,*
   your right hand will hold me fast.
¹¹ *If I say, "Surely the darkness will hide me*
   and the light become night around me,"
¹² *even the darkness will not be dark to you;*
   the night will shine like the day,
   for darkness is as light to you.
¹³ *For you created my inmost being;*
   you knit me together in my mother's womb.
¹⁴ *I praise you because I am fearfully and wonderfully made;*
   your works are wonderful,
   I know that full well.
¹⁵ *My frame was not hidden from you*
   when I was made in the secret place,
   when I was woven together in the depths of the earth.
¹⁶ *Your eyes saw my unformed body;*
   all the days ordained for me were written in your book
   before one of them came to be.
¹⁷ *How precious to me are your thoughts, God!*
   How vast is the sum of them!
¹⁸ *Were I to count them,*
   they would outnumber the grains of sand—
   when I awake, I am still with you.

> *¹⁹ If only you, God, would slay the wicked!*
>   *Away from me, you who are bloodthirsty!*
> *²⁰ They speak of you with evil intent;*
>   *your adversaries misuse your name.*
> *²¹ Do I not hate those who hate you, L*ORD*,*
>   *and abhor those who are in rebellion against you?*
> *²² I have nothing but hatred for them;*
>   *I count them my enemies.*
> *²³ Search me, God, and know my heart;*
>   *test me and know my anxious thoughts.*
> *²⁴ See if there is any offensive way in me,*
>   *and lead me in the way everlasting.*

We must examine ourselves. First, we must pray for God to reveal to us our own internal issues we need to deal with, then ask for His guidance and His plan for our lives. The second piece of fighting anger is explained in 1 Peter 3:8–17 (NIV), which says, "*⁸ Finally, all of you, be like-minded, be sympathetic, love one another, be compassionate and humble. ⁹ Do not repay evil with evil or insult with insult. On the contrary, repay evil with blessing, because to this you were called so that you may inherit a blessing. ¹⁰ For, 'Whoever would love life and see good days must keep their tongue from evil and their lips from deceitful speech. ¹¹ They must turn from evil and do good; they must seek peace and pursue it. ¹² For the eyes of the Lord are on the righteous and his ears are attentive to their prayer, but the face of the Lord is against those who do evil.' ¹³ Who is going to harm you if you are eager to do good? ¹⁴ But even if you should suffer for what is right, you are blessed. 'Do not fear their threats; do not be frightened.' ¹⁵ But in your hearts revere Christ as Lord. Always be prepared to give an answer to everyone who asks you to give the reason for the hope that you have. But do this with gentleness and respect, ¹⁶ keeping a clear conscience, so that those who speak maliciously against your good behavior in Christ may be ashamed of their slander. ¹⁷ For it is better, if it is God's will, to suffer for doing good than for doing evil.*"

I encourage you to read verses 18–22 of 1 Peter 3 as well. Peter proclaims that Jesus suffered for doing good, which ultimately was the perfect sacrifice for all the sins of humanity. Peter tells us that we should leave it up to God. Of course, we are going to suffer from doing bad, but we are also going to suffer for doing good sometimes. In my life, a lot of my anger comes from attempting to do good and being slighted in the process. In being honest, my anger also comes from God interrupting my plan, my selfish gain, or my agenda. It can also come from people interrupting good work because of their selfish gain or their personal agenda. Here's the thing: God does not promise that life will be easy and things will be handed to you. All people will suffer on Earth. As long as we can look in the mirror at the end of the day and think to ourselves, *I acted in good faith* or *I tried my hardest to do what God would have me to do,* we are suffering in Christ. He is suffering with us all over again.

Romans 8:18–27 (NIV):

"[18] *I consider that our present sufferings are not worth comparing with the glory that will be revealed in us.* [19] *For the creation waits in eager expectation for the children of God to be revealed.* [20] *For the creation was subjected to frustration, not by its own choice, but by the will of the one who subjected it, in hope* [21] *that the creation itself will be liberated from its bondage to decay and brought into the freedom and glory of the children of God.* [22] *We know that the whole creation has been groaning as in the pains of childbirth right up to the present time.* [23] *Not only so, but we ourselves, who have the firstfruits of the Spirit, groan inwardly as we wait eagerly for our adoption to sonship, the redemption of our bodies.* [24] *For in this hope we were saved. But hope that is seen is no hope at all. Who hopes for what they already have?* [25] *But if we hope for what we do not yet have, we wait for it patiently.* [26] *In the same way, the Spirit helps us in our weakness. We do not know what we ought to pray for, but the Spirit himself intercedes for us through wordless groans.* [27] *And he who searches our hearts knows the mind of the Spirit, because the Spirit intercedes for God's people in accordance with the will of God."*

The Bible promises us that we will face trials and tribulations. If you are looking for cupcakes and ponies every second of the day, following Christ is going to be a reality check for you. Regardless of whether your greatest sin is anger, as is mine, you will find there will always be something that will try to keep you from following Christ. We live in a world that is addicted to sin. We all relive the "fall of mankind" regularly. My struggle is my struggle. Your struggle, whatever it may be, is yours. We each have challenges in life. We all commit sin. As a matter of fact, the Bible tells us if we lie to ourselves and the rest of the world and say, "We are without sin," we make a liar out of God. That does not end well for anyone. 1 John 1:5–10 (NIV) are the verses I'm referring too. Think really hard about your life before committing to the phrase, "I do not sin." The verses read as follows:

"⁵ This is the message we have heard from him and declare to you: God is light; in him there is no darkness at all. ⁶ If we claim to have fellowship with him and yet walk in the darkness, we lie and do not live out the truth. ⁷ But if we walk in the light, as he is in the light, we have fellowship with one another, and the blood of Jesus, his Son, purifies us from all sin. ⁸ If we claim to be without sin, we deceive ourselves and the truth is not in us. ⁹ If we confess our sins, he is faithful and just and will forgive us our sins and purify us from all unrighteousness. ¹⁰ If we claim we have not sinned, we make him out to be a liar and his word is not in us."

Okay, now that we've gotten that out of the way and we agree we have all sinned and fallen short of the glory of God, let's take a look at a couple of popular lists of sins. You may be familiar with these lists, or not, but they have been pondered by many. Also, please note that these may not be the only sins out there. The Devil is crafty and likes to seek, kill, and destroy. In the article, "What Are The Seven Deadly Sins," the authors at *AllAboutGod* state that the seven deadly sins, or the seven detestable sins are:

Lust—to have an intense desire or need: *"But I tell you that anyone who looks at a woman lustfully has already committed adultery with her in his heart"* (Matthew 5:28).

Gluttony—excess in eating and drinking: *"for drunkards and gluttons become poor, and drowsiness clothes them in rags."* (Proverbs 23:21).

Greed—excessive or reprehensible acquisitiveness: *"Having lost all sensitivity, they have given themselves over to sensuality so as to indulge in every kind of impurity, with a continual lust for more."* (Ephesians 4:19).

Laziness—disinclined to activity or exertion; not energetic or vigorous: *"The way of the sluggard is blocked with thorns, but the path of the upright is a highway."* (Proverbs 15:19).

Wrath—strong vengeful anger or indignation: *"A gentle answer turns away wrath, but a harsh word stirs up anger."* (Proverbs 15:1)

Envy—painful or resentful awareness of an advantage enjoyed by another joined with a desire to possess the same advantage: *"Therefore, rid yourselves of all malice and all deceit, hypocrisy, envy, and slander of every kind. Like newborn babies, crave pure spiritual milk, so that by it you may grow up in your salvation"* (1 Peter 2:1–2).

Pride—quality or state of being proud; inordinate self-esteem: *"Pride goes before destruction, a haughty spirit before a fall."* (Proverbs 16:18).

Also, the seven detestable sins come from Proverbs 6:16–19 (NIV):
"There are six things the Lord hates, seven that are detestable to him: haughty eyes, a lying tongue, hands that shed innocent blood, a heart that devises wicked schemes, feet that are quick to rush into evil, a false witness who pours out lies and a man who stirs up dissension among brothers."

Regardless of the origins of these lists (that is a study in itself), they are both biblically based. One puts a term to the sin; the other is a straight verse from Proverbs 6. Either way, my point is that if you take a look at these lists, you cannot help but to think, *I don't do that one, I don't do that one, I know someone who did that one, I may do that one...* and so on. Let's be clear...are we judging? Yes. The question we need to ask ourselves is: are we judging others, or are we looking through the lens of Christ and saying, I (or someone I know of) may need help in this arena? It's so easy to look at these lists and judge.

These sins, whether or not you commit them, are sins. They are all about choice and how we choose to live our lives. We can choose to live our lives trying our best not to commit these sins, or we can give in and just live the way we want to. God gave us the freedom to choose. Either way, as we see with Judas' choices, God will use both good and bad in this world to do His will. His will always benefits His children. In this regard, we can learn from Judas' choices.

Did Judas betray Jesus strictly because of his pride? Maybe, maybe not. Take this into consideration: the day will come in your own life where you will come to a crossroads and have to decide which path to choose. One of my favorite quotes of all time is from the former New York Yankees' catcher, Yogi Berra. He once stated, "When you come to a fork in the road, take it." I know it doesn't make sense. It's either that or sheer brilliance. Either way, Yogi Berra was one of the best baseball players of all time, in my opinion.

It's a funny thing to think about, being predestined for something. Do you choose, or has your path been chosen for you already before you choose? Judas was called by Jesus, as were the rest of His disciples, as stated in Matthew. His sole purpose in this life was to betray the Son of Man. He chose to complete that destiny. Could he have chosen not to?

There are a few scriptures that may sway towards the side of "No, he really didn't have a choice." In Matthew 13:27 and Luke 22:3, we read, "Satan entered into him." I'm pretty sure that it was not Judas' intent to let Satan enter him. I could be wrong, but logically thinking it through, who would want Satan entering them? There are religions out there that worship the devil. The people of those religions may want Satan to enter them; I don't know, but from the text I believe we can determine that Judas did not fully choose it. Satan entering him was the larger part to his fall.

In Acts 1:16, we learned that David had prophesied about Judas in the Old Testament, as it states, "…and said, 'Brothers and sisters, the Scripture had to be fulfilled in which the Holy Spirit spoke long ago through David concerning Judas, who served as guide for those who arrested Jesus.'" Now, to my knowledge, I don't think Judas is called out anywhere in the Old Testament, but Acts does say that David prophesied the betrayal of Jesus by someone. Regardless of the exact wording, consider that someone was called to betray Jesus; Judas just made some bad choices leading him down the path of betraying Jesus.

In the days of Jesus' life, God had to hope no one would have to betray Jesus; that Judas would be with Him in Heaven along with the other disciples. God did not want humans to fall. It was the actions of Adam and Eve in the book of Genesis that set us, as a human race, up for failure. God gives us the ability to choose. But, God sees the best in people, even though He knows their outcome. The Bible tells us God is all-loving. He can love someone like Judas, even though He knew what Judas was going to do. God loves those who choose to walk the path of a destiny to fail, even though He knows they will one day fail.

Matthew 9 describes when Matthew was called, and while Jesus was dining at Matthew's house, the Pharisees asked Jesus, *"Why does your teacher eat with tax collectors and sinners?"* Jesus responded in verses 12–13 (NIV), saying, *"It is not the healthy who need a doctor, but the sick. ¹³ But go and learn what this means: 'I desire mercy, not sacrifice.' For I have not come to call the righteous, but sinners."*

God knows His children and knows who His children will be on the last day. Jesus knew that Judas would betray him but still loved him throughout the scripture. How can it be said that someone has a choice but in the same breath, say that someone is born with a purpose?

4

CHOOSING TO FOLLOW GOD

Paul, formally known as Saul

In Galatians 1, Paul realizes that he was called by God to minister to the Gentiles. Why is this important, you ask? Well, as you already know, prior to this, Paul was trying to destroy the Christian movement of the day. Judaism was his way of life prior to his epiphany on the road to Damascus.

Why would God take a man who was a well-known Pharisee and turn him into one of the men who wrote most of the New Testament? It's all about the testimony and the testament. Think about it. Jesus hung out with the worst of sinners. If he could turn their lives around, wouldn't that say more about him than having "good Christian" people follow him? Don't get me wrong, he still wants to attract good people as well. Have you ever heard someone tell a really cool story from their past and were like, "Wow! You have been through a lot," to the point of wanting to have experienced that same thing, so you can say you have done it too—right, wrong, or indifferent? The better the testimony, the better the testament of the power of God. Here is what we miss most of the time: God uses testimonies to influence society. He is going to work in people's lives no matter what we say or do. Sometimes we must allow God to work through our testimonies, but if we are afraid to share, or someone doesn't want to hear what we have to say, I guarantee you, God has other methods of reaching whom He pleases to reach; whom He has called to serve His will. In Paul's case, the people of the day knew who he had been and were able to see the physical/mental changes. Paul's life was a killer testimony filled with God's power.

Regardless of a major change in someone's life, or whether or not they have the greatest testimony on Earth, God desires to have a relationship with every living human being.

A Relationship with God

I once heard a definition of sin that I have found to be most fitting: "Committing an act that separates you from God." So many times in this life, we are called for so much more. Every single day of our lives, God wants to have a relationship with us. That, as human beings, is our part of God's plan. Sin keeps us from fulfilling that perfectly. Oftentimes our pride gets in the way, and we are stuck with the guilt that follows. We are separated from God, or so it seems.

So you ask yourself, how do I know I have a relationship with God? This seems like it would be an easy answer. Even after 30 years or so of having a relationship with God, some days I still question my relationship with Him. It would seem that a relationship with God would be like having a relationship with any other person. Any "good Christian" person would tell you it is. I'm here to tell you that if you feel confused about having a relationship with God, you're not alone. One thing that a relationship with God entails that all other relationships have is that it is a journey. It is a daily fight to keep that relationship going. I have a theory that all humans have an inkling built into their soul, by which they periodically want to try something new—whether that is daily, weekly, monthly, etc. We, as humans, desire to keep things interesting, or we simply get bored. Let me give you a little advice if you are feeling "the itch" to always do something new—don't. I can tell you from experience that looking for the latest and greatest thing to grab hold of leads to a harder life than what it should be. I'll give you an example from my own life.

Throughout my 10-year career with the U.S. Federal government, I have been in seven different jobs. I have been promoted multiple times throughout, but still seven jobs in ten years. God has brought this to my attention multiple times through multiple people. One thing that God is calling me to is contentment. It may not be your career; it may be moving from place to place or hopping from church to church. Though it is a way to live life, it is not how God would have us live our lives…or maybe it is. I would defer to God's calling on your life, rather than my opinion. For me, it's something I've been working on and will continue to work on in my walk with Christ. Why do I need to work on this, you ask? It interferes with a firm foundation with my career and with individuals I come in contact with. God's calling on our lives should never just be about the job, the church, or any physical possession; it's about the people and reaching those people. This is where my pride gets in the way of God's mission. This methodology affects my relationship with God and others.

Sorry for the tangent—let's get back to how you're supposed to know you have a relationship with God. I would submit to you that it is of your own threshold of how often you pray to God, read His word, and commune with others. There may be other things involved, but that is between you and God. Prayer is simply talking to God, but also should involve listening for what He is telling you. This is a huge difference in relationships with other humans. The Bible tells us that many folks have heard directly from God. They spoke to God like you and I would talk to each other. I mean, those who spoke to Jesus in His 33 years or so of the human form were talking directly to God, face-to-face. God still wants us to meet Him face-to-face. He desires a relationship with all of us, and a key part of that is simply talking to Him and listening, but we are all guilty of going and getting ourselves too busy to do so at some point or another. Sometimes we need to turn off the noise of this life and just have a chat with our Creator.

I have found that having a relationship with God is different for everyone. For one person, it may mean practicing a musical instrument. For someone else, it may mean playing a sport. For those of us who live in Washington D.C., it's praising and worshipping (and praying a lot) while sitting on any major freeway during rush hour traffic. The relationship you have with God is based on what your life looks like and what God's plan is for your life. It's also based on having a true foundation in Him, which is a balance of knowledge of what God's word says and living that out on a day-to-day basis.

God's plan has a purpose for your life and that purpose is between you and the Heavenly Father. There will come a day when you have to stand before the Lord and account for what you have done, and that conversation is going to be between you and Him. With that said, as a side note, someone may prophesy over you and have something to say about your life, but make sure it's 1) from God, and 2) isn't being used to manipulate you or your situation in any way. As there are false prophets in this world, you may ask, "How do I avoid becoming like Judas, or how do I protect my relationship with God? How do I protect myself from these false prophets?"

One must guard their heart against the attacks of the devil.

See, the devil is a schemer. He uses the things of this world to distract us and keep us from following the will of God. I would argue his best craft is the art of confusion. Take a minute and look back at your life, or maybe even your current situation, and notice how many answers are unclear about how you should proceed. I've found that when an answer seems like it should be simple, there are events that seem random that influence my decision. Frequently, those events bring confusion. Sometimes those events are from God and are guiding us through this world, but if you look closely and think hard about each event, you can tell which events brought you closer to God and which did not; which brought you to success versus which brought you damnation.

One thing that Judas failed miserably at was guarding his heart. As we know, Satan entered Judas before betraying Jesus. It may not have been his intent to allow Satan to enter into his life, but nonetheless, it happened, and Judas was held responsible for not guarding his heart. His failure to do so caused him to lose his family and friends, his lifestyle, his life itself, and ultimately, his soul.

Maintaining a well-fed relationship with God, of course, is not easy. It is hard work, and like any relationship, it takes time, sacrifice, and sometimes money. The concern we have for resources can be very overwhelming. Matthew chapter 6 explains a lot about how we should pray. Jesus, shortly after giving what is commonly known as "The Lord's Prayer" in Matthew 6:9–13, discusses the context of "worry." In Matthew 6, Jesus gives very clear instructions on how we should live our lives. I encourage you to read the full chapter, but to summarize, this chapter in whole touches on giving to the needy, prayer, fasting, storing up treasures in Heaven rather than on earth, and finally, worry—all very difficult areas of human nature.

First, giving away your money. Matthew 6:1–4 (NIV) says, *"1 Be careful not to practice your righteousness in front of others to be seen by them. If you do, you will have no reward from your Father in heaven. 2 So when you give to the needy, do not announce it with trumpets, as the hypocrites do in the synagogues and on the streets, to be honored by others. Truly I tell you, they have received their reward in full. 3 But when you give to the needy, do not let your left hand know what your right hand is doing, 4 so that your giving may be in secret. Then your Father, who sees what is done in secret, will reward you."*

This passage tells us that when we give, we should not take the credit. I have always been told (in church and at home) that my money and resources are not mine to begin with. God gives us the abilities, the talent, and the air we breathe to accomplish what we do in this life, whether it is something big or something small. This also gets into the reasons why we should tithe and give offering, but that is another message for another day. When we give, we should not be shouting it from the rooftops so as to draw attention to ourselves.

The second area Jesus talks about in Matthew 6 is prayer. In the scripture, there is not much of a segue between verses four and five, but it's Jesus talking here, so I wouldn't worry too much about it. Verses 5–14 include what is commonly known as "The Lord's Prayer." It is Jesus telling his disciples how they (we) should pray to God. Matthew 6:5–15 (NIV) says, *"⁵And when you pray, do not be like the hypocrites, for they love to pray standing in the synagogues and on the street corners to be seen by others. Truly I tell you, they have received their reward in full. ⁶ But when you pray, go into your room, close the door and pray to your Father, who is unseen. Then your Father, who sees what is done in secret, will reward you. ⁷ And when you pray, do not keep on babbling like pagans, for they think they will be heard because of their many words. ⁸ Do not be like them, for your Father knows what you need before you ask him. ⁹ This, then, is how you should pray: 'Our Father in heaven, hallowed be your name, ¹⁰ your kingdom come, your will be done, on earth as it is in heaven. ¹¹ Give us today our daily bread. ¹² And forgive us our debts, as we also have forgiven our debtors. ¹³ And lead us not into temptation, but deliver us from the evil one.' ¹⁴ For if you forgive other people when they sin against you, your heavenly Father will also forgive you. ¹⁵ But if you do not forgive others their sins, your Father will not forgive your sins.'"*

The Lord's Prayer touches on resources. Jesus tells us to pray for resources: "…give us today our daily bread." What I believe he is referring to are the resources we need, not the resources we desire. Nonetheless, it is okay to pray for resources. This prayer also touches on forgiveness. We must be forgiven to be in a relationship with God. In Matthew 18:21–35 (NIV), Jesus tells a parable about a servant who is unmerciful. He does not give the forgiveness he is given himself from his Master:

"²¹ Then Peter came to Jesus and asked, 'Lord, how many times shall I forgive my brother or sister who sins against me? Up to seven times?' ²² Jesus answered, 'I tell you, not seven times, but seventy-seven times.' ²³ Therefore, the kingdom of heaven is like a king who wanted to settle accounts with his servants. ²⁴ As he began the settlement, a man who owed him ten thousand bags of gold was brought to him.

²⁵ Since he was not able to pay, the master ordered that he and his wife and his children and all that he had be sold to repay the debt. ²⁶ At this the servant fell on his knees before him. 'Be patient with me,' he begged, 'and I will pay back everything.' ²⁷ The servant's master took pity on him, canceled the debt and let him go. ²⁸ But when that servant went out, he found one of his fellow servants who owed him a hundred silver coins. He grabbed him and began to choke him. 'Pay back what you owe me!' he demanded. ²⁹ His fellow servant fell to his knees and begged him, 'Be patient with me, and I will pay it back.' ³⁰ But he refused. Instead, he went off and had the man thrown into prison until he could pay the debt. ³¹ When the other servants saw what had happened, they were outraged and went and told their master everything that had happened. ³² Then the master called the servant in. 'You wicked servant,' he said, 'I canceled all that debt of yours because you begged me to. ³³ Shouldn't you have had mercy on your fellow servant just as I had on you?' ³⁴ In anger his master handed him over to the jailers to be tortured, until he should pay back all he owed. ³⁵ 'This is how my heavenly Father will treat each of you unless you forgive your brother or sister from your heart.'"

Forgiveness is also the keynote in this passage as Jesus said we should forgive someone 77 times, rather than the stated seven times Peter brings up. I like to think that Jesus was being sarcastic in this instance. When I read this, I like to believe that Jesus gave Peter a little attitude in this instance because he had been following him for some time in his ministry. It's one of those instances where Jesus would hit his forehead and say, "Come on, man, haven't you learned anything?" But Jesus has a lot more patience than I do, so of course, he answers how he answers.

From the passage, let's all be reminded here that the servant in the higher command position had the torture coming. I think that's all I have to say about that. Oh, and don't take that approach to management—it's rude. It's like throwing someone under the bus and not only running them over, but backing up over them, and running over them again. If you manage people in your day job or any other job for that matter, treat your people well. Part of this is forgiveness when they wrong you, but also that may mean them forgiving you or that you may need to forgive yourself.

We must forgive others, and sometimes, we need to learn to forgive ourselves. There was a time in my life where I didn't understand how to grasp the concept of being forgiven. In the church I grew up in, I was taught to forgive others. No one ever told me I needed to forgive myself. There is a misnomer in the modern church, which is that we must be forgiven by God (which is true), and we must forgive others to be forgiven (which is true), but what is lacking in that statement is we sometimes need to forgive ourselves as well. There will be times in your life where you are so disgusted by yourself and the things you have done. This disgust can come in many different forms: addiction, self-harm, harm done to others, etc. Whatever you have done, wherever you have been, and anything that you have seen, can all be erased by God. He can make you new. It all starts with forgiveness of others and forgiveness of self.

"Forgive us our debts, as we also have forgiven our debtors. And lead us not in temptation, but deliver us from the evil one." And I like how the King James Version ends verse 13: "For thine is the kingdom, and the power, and the glory, forever. Amen." Don't ask why the NIV version does not include this. Just one of those things, I guess. I wouldn't focus on it too much. I like to think that the folks that wrote the New International Version of the Bible are proposing that we never end our prayers, and we are in constant prayer with God, whereas the KJV folks end prayers and stop at certain points. But who am I to say? Regardless, we have to forgive.

Verses 16–18 cover fasting. The Bible mentions a couple of times when Jesus fasted. Fasting is one of those things that has changed over time. In my experience, like everything else in this world, it has become more commercialized in the last couple of decades. I want to encourage you to keep fasting, to truly fast whenever possible, but do it in such a way that no one knows about it. It's meant to be something sacred between you and God. Corporate fasting is a thing. The Bible speaks of it a couple of times in Nehemiah 9, Joel 1:14, etc. where a group of people gathered in a fast. I want to encourage you to be mindful of how you approach corporate fasting. I believe the same rules apply to people gathering to fast, as Jesus lays out in Matthew 6:16-18 (NIV):

"16 When you fast, do not look somber as the hypocrites do, for they disfigure their faces to show others they are fasting. Truly I tell you, they have received their reward in full. 17 But when you fast, put oil on your head and wash your face, 18 so that it will not be obvious to others that you are fasting, but only to your Father, who is unseen; and your Father, who sees what is done in secret, will reward you."

After you have given to the needy, prayed, and fasted, then we can work on our savings account—in Heaven that is. Verses 19–24 speak of remaining spiritually healthy and making good decisions to live for Christ. These are some of my favorite verses in the Bible, simply because it tells us of what to come for our suffering here on Earth. These verses are a warning to all. Watch out for your lust, and you can't love God and money. But then once you have worked through this process, you will be relieved of worry.

Matthew 6:25–34 discusses worry and how we should handle that. Let me tell you, we don't need to handle a thing. We are supposed to give it up to God. I've always thought of it this way: God created the heavens and the earth in seven days, so I'm pretty sure He can handle anything you are going through in this life. This chapter shows us that when we give, when we pray, when we fast, when we store up our treasure in Heaven rather than on Earth, when we give our worrying to God, then God will move in our lives. We will find His plan for our lives. Our earthly resources aren't ours in the first place, nor can we take them with us when we die. No matter how you play it, this world is going to keep everything you have. However, the next world will have everything you desire if you continually seek God and choose His path. Now, Matthew 6 makes it seem easy. In case you're thinking, *Yeah Jordan, I'll just do those five things, and all will be good. I'll be good to go to Heaven.* Well, there's this thing referred to as sinful nature, remember? And we just so happen to be human. So how do we control that sinful nature and move towards the plan God has for our lives?

DO NOT MAKE YOUR SIN THE MAIN FOCUS OF YOUR LIFE.

So many times in life, we put too much focus on sin. What does that do for us? Well, if you focus on something, you give that thing attention—you give it life. This is important to know, especially for those deeply rooted sins that we feel we may never stop committing. We all have our road to Damascus. Following God or not, we all get a "light" from God telling us to go certain ways in life. No matter how worldly someone becomes, they still have God-moments in their life. Some have chosen to accept those moments in their life and turn to God's plan for their life. Others continue to disregard it. And yet others don't acknowledge them as moments given to them by God. If you continually choose to make your sin the focus of your life, you will never fully understand what your true calling is. You will never understand when your road to Damascus moment comes into your life. It may be a miracle; it may be some thing or person you cannot explain. But one day, it will come, and we need to be ready to accept that it is truly God acting out His plan for our lives. Another way of going about losing out on the "Road to Damascus" moment is by running when you clearly know what God wants you to do in your life. Take Jonah, for instance.

Jonah was prejudiced towards the people of Nineveh. He did not want them to be saved, so much so that he told God to kill him rather than make him go to Nineveh. Jonah 1:1–3 (NIV) states, *"¹ The word of the Lord came to Jonah son of Amittai: ² 'Go to the great city of Nineveh and preach against it, because its wickedness has come up before me.' ³ But Jonah ran away from the Lord and headed for Tarshish. He went down to Joppa, where he found a ship bound for that port. After paying the fare, he went aboard and sailed for Tarshish to flee from the Lord."*

Of course, we all know the story. He is floating along, and a huge storm is going to capsize the boat. He tells the other folks to throw him in, and the storm will calm. They do, and the storm calms. He gets swallowed by a big fish. The big fish spits him out after three days, and he ends up going to Nineveh. He preached to the people of Nineveh, they repented from their evil ways, and God spared them. This is a summarized version of Jonah chapters 1–3. Jonah chapter 4 is a different story. This is the "adult version" of the Bible that the Sunday School teachers would always leave out growing up as a kid. In Jonah chapter 4, Jonah is angry with God for saving the people of Nineveh. He feels it's unfair, so much so that he wants to die. Jonah goes out to the desert and basically argues with God about how he is angry with the way God handled the city of Nineveh. God sends a plant to give Jonah shade, and then the next night, a bug comes and eats the plant. The plant then dies and withers away. Jonah was angry about the plant dying and tells God once again to take his life. God tells Jonah this in verses 10–11 (NIV): *"¹⁰ But the Lord said, 'You have been concerned about this plant, though you did not tend it or make it grow. It sprang up overnight and died overnight. ¹¹ And should I not have concern for the great city of Nineveh, in which there are more than a hundred and twenty thousand people who cannot tell their right hand from their left—and also many animals?'"*

Jonah could have been happy for God saving the people of Nineveh. It was a great victory for God's Kingdom. Instead, he pouted about it. We don't know what happened to Jonah after that. The book of Jonah is only four chapters, after all. All we know is that he was angry about the people of Nineveh being saved by God all four chapters. Even though he kicked and screamed the entire time, God still used him to save 120,000 people or so. Jonah had served his purpose in life. God used him the way God can use any one of us. It was God's plan to save the people of Nineveh, one way or the other. Jonah could have died at sea with the rest of the folks on the boat if he hadn't told them to throw him overboard. I guarantee you that God would have sent someone else to Nineveh. For some reason, God wanted the people of Nineveh saved. Jonah had his pride to get over, as well as his prejudice towards the Ninevites. In today's society, there are so many disruptions and distractions that can move us away from God, or at the time, seem to move us away from God. He never leaves our side, as long as we choose to keep coming back to Him.

5
THE TRUE MYSTERY OF GOD'S PLAN

Disruptions. God often uses disruption to alter our paths. Why does He allow disruptions to happen to us? Is He some Big Guy up in the sky toying around with human beings for His own pleasure? Let's remember that God loves us, first and foremost. God disrupts our lives because He knows what's best for us. He knows how our lives are going to end up before we are finished living them. Before we have fully lived each second, each minute, each hour, each day, each week, each month, each quarter (for all you business-related folks out there), each year, each decade, etc., He knows what is going to happen. He knows how we will choose and what paths we will take. He knows who His children are; He knows who His chosen are. He knows how we will react to something before we even react. This is the mystery of God. He knows what we will choose before we choose, but He also lets us choose what we are going to choose. God does not control our choices. He allows for disruptions. He allows for the good and the bad to happen to us, as to hope that we will choose Him every time.

Do you ever wonder why some things happen the way they do? Why the order of events occurs in the order they do? If God has a plan for us, why then do we have to be put through certain circumstances? There are many reasons for the order of events. For example, say a person is applying for a job. The order of events may go something like this:

Search for jobs
Find the job of interest
Fill out an application for the job of interest
Receive a call from the hiring organization
Set up an interview
Go to the interview
Crush the interview (because let's face it, you're awesome!)
Fill out human resources paperwork for the job
Start the job
Love the job

Then again, this isn't a perfect world. Instead of the ten items listed above, there are plenty of different scenarios that could play out. The same scenario could look something like this:

Search for jobs; take two weeks to find the job of interest.

Find the job of interest; debate for a couple of days whether or not you should apply; this could include many thoughts, lack of sleep if you're excited about it, talking to friends and family about the job of interest, anxiety that you're not qualified for the job of interest, etc.

Fill out an application for the job of interest; depending on the job, this could take many days, or even multiple days of research.

Receive a call from the hiring organization; this could take weeks, months, years…

Set up an interview; hopefully, this only takes one phone call with the Human Resource folks.

Go to the interview; you're probably nervous, excited, and rehearsing over and over what to say and trying to go through every question the interviewer could possibly ask you.

Crush the interview (because let's face it, you're awesome!); Maybe, or maybe not (just remember you're human, after all).

Fill out human resources paperwork for the job; assuming you got the job and didn't bomb the interview

Start the job; this could be, or maybe they found someone else, someone better than you.

Love the job; did you ever stop and question, "Did God want you to have this job? Was it part of His plan for you?"

So many times, we think we know what is best for our lives. God gives us the freedom to choose in this life. But say, you stop before step one of that job opportunity process and ask yourself, "What does God want for my life?" I like how James puts it in James 4:13–17 (ESV) when he says, *"[13] Come now, you who say, 'Today or tomorrow we will go into such and such a town and spend a year there and trade and make a profit'—[14] yet you do not know what tomorrow will bring. What is your life? For you are a mist that appears for a little time and then vanishes. [15] Instead you ought to say, 'If the Lord wills, we will live and do this or that.' [16] As it is, you boast in your arrogance. All such boasting is evil. [17] So whoever knows the right thing to do and fails to do it, for him it is sin."*

We all want to be successful in life. We want to leave some sort of legacy, whether that is a position or title, family, the way we have to live our life, etc. How success is measured comes down to the individual. Regardless of how it's measured, some folks put way too much pressure on themselves to meet their goals. Some do not apply enough pressure on themselves to meet their goals. Whatever you define as your legacy, consider this: It's not yours; let it go. God has a plan for your life. Whether you choose to or not, you're going to follow His path or an alternative path; you choose a path. However you choose, God will still make the outcome, in some way, shape, or form, bring glory to Him. James 4 covers this concept. It explains to us how if we choose our own path and it doesn't align with God's path, we have committed sin. Like a child disobeying their parents, it is a sin. You have a choice to bring glory to God through your life or not. I encourage you to choose the right path—God's path.

Take, for instance, Cain, in the book of Genesis. Genesis 4 tells us the story of Cain and Able, the first two sons of Adam and Eve. Cain did not bring forth the appropriate sacrifices to God, but Able did. Therefore, God gave favor to Able, not Cain (verses 6–7). Cain became jealous of Able and killed him, marking him as the first murderer to walk the earth. At this time, God was still talking to Cain. God's will for Cain's life (bringing the right items to sacrifice) was changed based on Cain's decision to bring the wrong sacrifices. Instead, Cain was banished to an outlandish city where he lived out the rest of his life, away from the people who loved and cared for him (who brought him joy). Cain let his sin control his life, and he paid the lifetime punishment for his actions. The Bible does not tell us if he spent eternity in Hell, but it does say that Adam and Eve had a son to replace Able's purpose—Seth—and that the bloodline of Seth were those who continued to call on the name of the Lord. The purpose that God had for Cain and Able ended up being fulfilled by Seth. Life could have been different...

There have been times in this life when door after door gets slammed in our faces. If you are one of God's chosen, you have a higher calling in your life to believe in something greater than day-to-day activities and day-to-day problems. In the second "job" scenario, what if God's plan was for you to interview, but not get the position? An even harder pill to swallow is, what if what you thought God's plan was for you to land the job, then at the last minute, the company chooses someone else for the position? It's okay to be angry, but just know that God has a plan that does not have you in that job. I challenge you to read the Book of Revelation. When you read it, come at it with a mindset of, if this is going to happen, if this is God's end to the world, then why shouldn't I trust in what comes in the middle? See, we are in the "middle stage" of God's plan. God gave us the beginning in the

Book of Genesis. He gave us the end in the Book of Revelation. If we have the beginning and the end already spelled out for us, does it really matter what is in the middle? Yes! Every piece of God's plan leads up to the end of time. Even if someone is not a part of the body of Christ, their actions make up "the middle." Just imagine how many pieces of people's lives have to align for you to land a job. I listed some, but not all, in the examples. That is just one tiny piece of what goes on in this world on a daily basis. Imagine how many people are going through the job hiring process at any given time in the world. Thousands, if not millions, on a daily basis.

To God, your one little job search, your one little application, your one little job interview, and your one little job matters in His plan. Think about how many people you come into contact with because of your job on a daily basis, and how many transactions you make that affect the lives of others. Can you put a number on it? Sometimes it's not about the job. Sometimes it's about what you learn through that experience. Sometimes it's about touching people's lives and simply being an example for them. Sometimes it's about being coachable so your supervisor is able to teach you. As much as we think we do, we will never see the full picture. Some can see more of the picture than others, but never the "full" picture. God can see the full picture. Can God use disruptions in our lives for His good? Absolutely. It is the acceptance or the denial of God's true plan that determines what happens next. Whatever happens, one day, there will be an end to this world. Don't worry, the good guys win. Bringing it back around to Judas and how his choices affected this world (because we're all thinking about our own actions for a moment), did Judas have a choice in betraying Jesus, or was it predetermined?

To answer these questions, we must consider Old Testament scripture. More specifically, the books that reference Israel's falling-outs from God. For example, the people of Israel worshipping the golden calf in the desert under Moses' command after God had clearly just saved them from the Egyptians and provided for their needs in the desert.

Other examples come from books like Nehemiah and Amos, where God is looking to destroy the Israelites because they are being terrible people in sinning tremendously, along with their surrounding neighbors. These books list out the times the Israelites have disobeyed God, and the times their ancestors disobeyed God. Sometimes they get so repetitive, at least for me, there is a temptation to glance over the reading. If you don't get the same temptation, well, you're just a better Christian than me. Anyway, back to the purpose. These books deliver a message of the strength of God. They deliver a piece of the puzzle that I believe is pertinent to our discussion. If God's chosen people (Israel, as claimed in the Bible on multiple occasions) can disobey God, and He continually accepts them, we are able to do the same. I'm not saying we should try to sin, but we have the ability to act on our own behalf and ask God for forgiveness. Even though it worked a little differently in those days (i.e., burnt offerings for forgiveness), they could also be forgiven of their sins.

Then in stories from the Bible like Daniel facing the lion's den; Shadrach, Meshach, and Abednego being thrown into the fiery furnace; Job being tested by Satan, etc., where the individual(s) of the story are trusting God throughout the entire story, knowing that at the worst time, God will show up for them. Those individuals showed discipline in God's plan. They committed to living a life for God. They did not back away from trusting in God, even in the most difficult of circumstances. Comparatively, for example, Jonah fled because he didn't want to go to Nineveh, whereas Daniel would not bow down to the king, but only to God. The end result for both Jonah and Daniel were similar. They both ended up in places they did not want to be (the belly of a fish and a lion's den). The difference is that Jonah had some regret on the way he approached things, while Daniel did not. Jonah lacked discipline, initially, while Daniel did not. The Bible tells us in Hebrews 12:11 (NIV) that *"No discipline seems pleasant at the time, but painful. Later on, however, it produces a harvest of righteousness and peace for those who have been trained by it."*

I'll bet that Daniel had peace the rest of his life for how he handled his situation. Jonah may have had some demons to face by how he handled his. Regardless, I'm going to go out on a limb and say we will see them both in Heaven one day because whether you go kicking and screaming or you are disciplined in your faith, God has a plan for you. The passage into Heaven is simple: Believe that Jesus Christ died on the cross for your sins, try your best to follow the guidance of the Bible throughout your life, and love others.

6

CHOOSE TO BE CHOSEN

God's chosen...

The ultimate example of being God's chosen is, of course, Jesus Christ. He is the Son of God, who is God, as part of the Holy Trinity. He was sent to this earth to be a sacrifice for the sins of the people. To be the intercession, we, as sinners, needed to interact with God the Father. The prophet Isaiah envisioned the coming of Jesus to the earth and gave a clear picture of how it would all go down. Isaiah 53 (ESV) explains the coming of Christ as such:

> [1] *Who has believed what he has heard from us?*
> *And to whom has the arm of the Lord been revealed?*
> [2] *For he grew up before him like a young plant,*
> *and like a root out of dry ground;*
> *he had no form or majesty that we should look at him,*
> *and no beauty that we should desire him.*
> [3] *He was despised and rejected by men,*
> *a man of sorrows and acquainted with grief;*
> *and as one from whom men hide their faces*
> *he was despised, and we esteemed him not.*
> *Surely he has borne our griefs*
> *and carried our sorrows;*
> *yet we esteemed him stricken,*

JORDAN M. RIEDEL

    smitten by God, and afflicted.
⁵ *But he was pierced for our transgressions;*
    he was crushed for our iniquities;
upon him was the chastisement that brought us peace,
    and with his wounds we are healed.
⁶ *All we like sheep have gone astray;*
    we have turned—every one—to his own way;
and the Lord has laid on him
    the iniquity of us all.
⁷ *He was oppressed, and he was afflicted,*
    yet he opened not his mouth;
like a lamb that is led to the slaughter,
    and like a sheep that before its shearers is silent,
    so he opened not his mouth.
⁸ *By oppression and judgment he was taken away;*
    and as for his generation, who considered
that he was cut off out of the land of the living,
    stricken for the transgression of my people?
⁹ *And they made his grave with the wicked*
    and with a rich man in his death,
although he had done no violence,
    and there was no deceit in his mouth.
¹⁰ *Yet it was the will of the Lord to crush him;*
    he has put him to grief;
when his soul makes an offering for guilt,
    he shall see his offspring; he shall prolong his days;
the will of the Lord shall prosper in his hand.
¹¹ *Out of the anguish of his soul he shall see and be satisfied;*
by his knowledge shall the righteous one, my servant,
    make many to be accounted righteous,
    and he shall bear their iniquities.
¹² *Therefore I will divide him a portion with the many,*
    and he shall divide the spoil with the strong,
because he poured out his soul to death
    and was numbered with the transgressors;
yet he bore the sin of many,
    and makes intercession for the transgressors.

CHOSEN

Jesus came to fulfill the will of God. The will of God was for him to suffer at the hands of humans, so he could save all who would accept Him for what he is—love. God gave Jesus a choice, as a human, to go through with it. Of course, we all know the ending to that story, but Jesus had a choice to fulfill the will of God. Jesus is God; He was God from the beginning. He knew the end before the start of all the pain. He saw the vision of the success that would come from His acts. In 2 Peter 1:3–11 (NIV), as God's elect, God inspired Peter to give us guidelines on how to act as God's elect:

"*3 His divine power has given us everything we need for a godly life through our knowledge of him who called us by his own glory and goodness. 4 Through these he has given us his very great and precious promises, so that through them you may participate in the divine nature, having escaped the corruption in the world caused by evil desires. 5 For this very reason, make every effort to add to your faith goodness; and to goodness, knowledge; 6 and to knowledge, self-control; and to self-control, perseverance; and to perseverance, godliness; 7 and to godliness, mutual affection; and to mutual affection, love. 8 For if you possess these qualities in increasing measure, they will keep you from being ineffective and unproductive in your knowledge of our Lord Jesus Christ. 9 But whoever does not have them is nearsighted and blind, forgetting that they have been cleansed from their past sins. 10 Therefore, my brothers and sisters, make every effort to confirm your calling and election. For if you do these things, you will never stumble, 11 and you will receive a rich welcome into the eternal kingdom of our Lord and Savior Jesus Christ.*"

As God's elect, God has commanded us to love each other despite the circumstance. To act as Jesus did when he was being nailed to a tree in the middle of a middle-eastern countryside, named Golgotha or "skull." If we surrender ourselves to God's will, we become God's elect by the relationship we build with Him. By which, we will become justified in what we do. We become justified by His grace and mercy. We become heirs to the Kingdom of God. In Titus 3:1–8 (NIV), the Bible explains how we might be saved:

"¹ Remind the people to be subject to rulers and authorities, to be obedient, to be ready to do whatever is good, ² to slander no one, to be peaceable and considerate, and always to be gentle toward everyone. ³ At one time we too were foolish, disobedient, deceived and enslaved by all kinds of passions and pleasures. We lived in malice and envy, being hated and hating one another. ⁴ But when the kindness and love of God our Savior appeared, ⁵ he saved us, not because of righteous things we had done, but because of his mercy. He saved us through the washing of rebirth and renewal by the Holy Spirit, ⁶ whom he poured out on us generously through Jesus Christ our Savior, ⁷ so that, having been justified by his grace, we might become heirs having the hope of eternal life. ⁸ This is a trustworthy saying. And I want you to stress these things, so that those who have trusted in God may be careful to devote themselves to doing what is good. These things are excellent and profitable for everyone."

In this life, there are voids no person or thing can fill. There is a void that can only be filled by the one, true God. And yet, we deny Him this place in our lives. We try to fill it with worldly things; the desires of our hearts. We try to own our own lives and are continually unsuccessful. There is no answer in this world for the void that only God can fill. As hard as we try, we will never be God, nor will we come close. We will continue to walk aimlessly through life, searching and seeking to fill the void. When we completely surrender our lives to Christ, this void will be no more.

II Timothy 2:11–13 (NIV) says, *"¹¹ Here is a trustworthy saying: If we died with him, we will also live with him; ¹² if we endure, we will also reign with him. If we disown him, he will also disown us; ¹³ if we are faithless, he remains faithful, for he cannot disown himself."*

Perhaps we need to start looking to God to fill our every gap in life. We need Him to fill the holes that no human can patch up and repair. We need Him to reluctantly give us breath so we can continue to breathe. We need God simply to live, to keep going in this life. Therefore, if you want to be the "Chosen

People," 1 Peter 2:1–10 (NIV) gives us the encouragement on how to go about that"

"¹ Therefore, rid yourselves of all malice and all deceit, hypocrisy, envy, and slander of every kind. ² Like newborn babies, crave pure spiritual milk, so that by it you may grow up in your salvation, ³ now that you have tasted that the Lord is good. The Living Stone and a Chosen People: ⁴ As you come to him, the living Stone—rejected by humans but chosen by God and precious to him—⁵ you also, like living stones, are being built into a spiritual house to be a holy priesthood, offering spiritual sacrifices acceptable to God through Jesus Christ. ⁶ For in Scripture it says: 'See, I lay a stone in Zion, a chosen and precious cornerstone, and the one who trusts in him will never be put to shame.' ⁷ Now to you who believe, this stone is precious. But to those who do not believe, 'The stone the builders rejected has become the cornerstone,' ⁸ and, 'A stone that causes people to stumble and a rock that makes them fall.' They stumble because they disobey the message—which is also what they were destined for. ⁹ But you are a chosen people, a royal priesthood, a holy nation, God's special possession, that you may declare the praises of him who called you out of darkness into his wonderful light. ¹⁰ Once you were not a people, but now you are the people of God; once you had not received mercy, but now you have received mercy."

50/50

Peter gives the analogy of Jesus being a living stone, and if we draw near to him, we will be of a royal priesthood. There is a common message found throughout the Bible of how God describes how people are looked at destined to:

1) Be of God: One who accepts of his call. A person of His royal priesthood. One who accepts Him as the cornerstone.

2) Be not of God: One who rejects of his call. A person who disobeys His word. One who rejects Him as the

cornerstone, and places something else in this world, as their cornerstone.

Likewise, the Bible explains this simple phenomenon of which it will also be in the last days of life on this earth. Typically, the story has two people in it doing similar things; one is taken, and one is left behind. Hence, the name 50/50. Please do not take the straight concept that you have a 50% chance of making it into Heaven. Rather, consider the difficulty. Take Judas Iscariot, for instance. The man followed Christ (who was and is, and is to be, as best as I can humanly describe it, "perfection") for three years—stood next to Him for approximately 1,095 days (according to the modern-day calendar). For approximately 26,280 hours, he walked with him, ate with him, slept next to him. He had it easier than large majority or people throughout time to follow God's will, but still chose the world.

The ideology of 50/50 is not based on one person, but of many. When the Bible talks about "one being taken, one being left," the authors (inspired by God) were trying to explain the concept of God's chosen being reunited with Christ again. This does not mean you have a 50% chance of having a relationship with God; it's simply saying you have a choice: Do you want to be taken and reunited with Christ, in Heaven, or do you want to be left to this earth and sent to an eternity in Hell?

In this life, it's very easy to "miss the mark." How easy it is to walk with Jesus one day, then have your life take a 180-degree turn for the worse, the next. Jesus spells out what the end times will look like in Matthew 24.

Jesus warns believers not to be deceived (Matthew 24:5–9 (NIV)). For Example, *"⁵ For many will come in my name, claiming, 'I am the Messiah,' and will deceive many. ⁶ You will hear of wars and rumors of wars, but see to it that you are not alarmed. Such things must happen, but the end is still to come. ⁷ Nation will rise against nation, and kingdom against kingdom. There will be famines and earthquakes in various places. ⁸ All these are the beginning of birth pains. ⁹ Then you will be handed over to be persecuted and put to death, and you will be hated by all nations because of me."* The text goes on in verse 13 to say, *"Those who stand firm will be saved."* Those who stand firm are God's chosen; they are God's elect.

In verse 24, Jesus continues by saying in those days, even the elect will be deceived by the false prophets and false messiahs. Then once the Son of Man reappears, the angels "will collect" the chosen. Then, in verses 36–41 (NIV), Jesus gives the reader "the kicker":

"^{36}*But about that day or hour no one knows, not even the angels in heaven, nor the Son, but only the Father.* ^{37}*As it was in the days of Noah, so it will be at the coming of the Son of Man.* ^{38}*For in the days before the flood, people were eating and drinking, marrying and giving in marriage, up to the day Noah entered the ark;* ^{39}*and they knew nothing about what would happen until the flood came and took them all away. That is how it will be at the coming of the Son of Man.* ^{40}*Two men will be in the field; one will be taken and the other left.* ^{41}*Two women will be grinding with a hand mill; one will be taken and the other left."*

God gives us a picture of the end times and some things to look for during those times. Matthew 24 is that picture. If you are a believer, these signs will be clear; you will be ridiculed and hated for your faith, especially if you are God's elect. Sounds awesome! God also encourages us by explaining that it's temporary, and these times will be shortened for his elect. Regardless of what these times look like for any given person or group of persons, they will happen, and no one person knows when they will happen. So don't worry, it's all going to be okay; the good guys win in the end. It is up to your choices on whether or not you are one of the good guys.

God's true hope is that His elect will "keep watch" and not fall into the trap of the Devil. He makes this clear in the following verses (42–51). It is spelled out that no one will know the hour that the Son of Man returns to Earth; he will come "like a thief," aka someone or something you do not expect or see coming. The point here is that no one knows when Jesus is coming back. There will and have been people in the world who claim to know the exact date that Jesus will return. Even if you are not a Christian, if someone tells you when the world is going to end, please at least second-guess them and fact check them. We can all look at Matthew 24, even if it is just for a historical reference.

As for God's elect, "Keep Watch" for the day of the Lord will come, and all you have to do is be prepared for it to happen. If you truly believe you are not God's elect and you would like to become His elect, simply commit your life to Christ (believe Jesus died on the cross for your salvation) and turn from your sins. You have two options, "A" or "B," "right" or "wrong," yes or no, Satan or God, Life or Death—50/50.

FORGIVENESS

In Luke 17:26–37 (NIV), we see some of the same language about the final day. For example, Luke spells out what happened in the days of Noah, and the day the flood came, as does Matthew. But he continues with a slightly different message to the reader in verse 33:

"*26 Just as it was in the days of Noah, so also will it be in the days of the Son of Man. 27 People were eating, drinking, marrying and being given in marriage up to the day Noah entered the ark. Then the flood came and destroyed them all. 28 It was the same in the days of Lot. People were eating and drinking, buying and selling, planting and building. 29 But the day Lot left Sodom, fire and sulfur rained down from heaven and destroyed them all. 30 It will be just like this on the day the Son of Man is revealed. 31 On that day no one who is on the housetop, with possessions inside, should go down to get them. Likewise, no one in the field should go back for anything. 32 Remember Lot's wife! 33 Whoever tries to keep their life will lose it, and whoever loses their life will preserve it. 34 I tell you, on that night two people will be in one bed; one will be taken and the other left. 35 Two women will be grinding grain together; one will be taken and the other left." [36] 37 'Where, Lord?' they asked. He replied, 'Where there is a dead body, there the vultures will gather.'"

Luke describes a person who tries to keep their life and a person who loses their life. The one who tries to keep their life is a person who holds on to the things of this world. When I read this verse, it always makes me think of the clothing brand "Not of This World." God does not want us to hold on to this world. He wants us to always be looking to Heaven (God's elects' final resting place). It is called out in the Bible on several occasions, in different ways (i.e., go back and read Matthew 24:35 for just a second, then continue reading this. Also, another reference is Luke 21:33). "Heaven and Earth shall pass away" is how it is referred to in these two scriptures. Regardless of how the scriptures spell it out, God wants us to know that Earth is temporary. One day, either by your own death, or the coming of the Lord, it will be gone. And you can't take your stuff with you. The message here that Luke is trying to get at is to "let this life go" or "lose your life" because that is the only way to become God's elect.

In 1 Thessalonians 4:13–18 (NIV), we read:

"13 Brothers and sisters, we do not want you to be uninformed about those who sleep in death, so that you do not grieve like the rest of mankind, who have no hope. 14 For we believe that Jesus died and rose again, and so we believe that God will bring with Jesus those who have fallen asleep in him. 15 According to the Lord's word, we tell you that we who are still alive, who are left until the coming of the Lord, will certainly not precede those who have fallen asleep. 16 For the Lord himself will come down from heaven, with a loud command, with the voice of the archangel and with the trumpet call of God, and the dead in Christ will rise first. 17 After that, we who are still alive and are left will be caught up together with them in the clouds to meet the Lord in the air. And so we will be with the Lord forever. 18 Therefore encourage one another with these words."

I have always read this and thought, *is the Bible contradicting itself?* Then I remember shortly thereafter that it is the inspired word of God, and everything in the Bible has a purpose. Sometimes the different translations of the Bible from the original text is confusing, but theologians could explain this concept to you better than I can. In this case, the "Dead in Christ" are folks that are actually dead on Earth but lived a life for Christ. That's my best guess; take it for what it is. This passage talks about everyone who will rise with Christ on the last day (God's elect). Once again, we see a comparison of those who make it into Heaven and those who do not. People that are "sleeping in death" are those who have no hope. Meaning, they are lost souls. Regardless of which side of the coin people fall on, the Bible calls us to encourage one another with these words as God's elect.

I grew up in the church. From an early age, I was told, "Ask Jesus for forgiveness, by believing in your heart that Jesus died for your sins, and you will make it into Heaven." I never really understood the concept of why I needed to be forgiven until I began looking into it myself around the age of ten. So many times, we get caught up in believing what our earthly parents believe. When, in fact—and I love my parents very much—our parents (or parental figures) on Earth don't always know everything that is best for us. In this case, I was fortunate to have parents that took me to church almost every Sunday growing up. I'm not saying that growing up in the church automatically gets you into Heaven because that is nowhere close to the truth, but it helped me learn how to become God's elect. The simple answer to the question, "How does one become God's Elect?" can be found in the most popular verse in the Bible. This is, of course, John 3:16 (NIV). *"For God so loved the world that he gave his one and only Son, that whoever believes in him shall not perish but have eternal life."*

First, with this popular verse, we can see that it is by choice that we believe in Christ and the sacrifice He made for our sins. This is good news for all who do not know Jesus and feel like they have no chance of getting into Heaven. There is, and always will be, a solution. Simply, believe in Jesus/God/the Holy Spirit and that God sent Jesus to die on the cross as a sacrifice for your sins and mine; so that we may be forgiven. How do we become God's Elect? We make the choice to accept Christ as our savior and to be FORGIVEN.

I will say, even as a lifelong Christian, I have struggled to grasp the concept of forgiveness. As simple as it sounds, it is rather difficult to perform. We are forgiven many times throughout our lives and God gives us peace about sinning in verses such as Matthew 11:28–30 (NIV). It says, *"[28] Come to me, all you who are weary and burdened, and I will give you rest. [29] Take my yoke upon you and learn from me, for I am gentle and humble in heart, and you will find rest for your souls. [30] For my yoke is easy and my burden is light."* Being God's chosen is simply being forgiven and accepting that forgiveness; even when it is yourself that you must forgive.

In the end, each person will have to answer for their life. Revelation 20:11–12 (KJV) tells us:

"[11] And I saw a great white throne, and him that sat on it, from whose face the earth and the heaven fled away; and there was found no place for them. [12] And I saw the dead, small and great, stand before God; and the books were opened: and another book was opened, which is the book of life: and the dead were judged out of those things which were written in the books, according to their works."

Each person who has lived in this world will one day stand before the one true God. They will be judged for everything they have ever done. Jesus tells us in John 5:24 that those who hear His word and believe it will have everlasting life will not come into condemnation, but are passed from death to life; believers of Christ will not suffer, but will go to Heaven. I cannot speak for anyone else's life, nor how they live it, but when I was a child, I said the sinner's prayer hundreds, maybe even thousands of times. I wanted to make sure I was going to Heaven. I question now if I truly understood what I was saying. Eventually, I grew out of saying the sinner's prayer over and over again when I learned how asking for forgiveness is supposed to be sincere and from the heart. It is not only simple words to mutter over and over again, though sometimes I do feel like that is what we need and/or what God needs from us. It took years for me to understand that God forgives us when we, as His children, ask for forgiveness. When we feel guilt, it's Satan trying to hold us down from growing in the Lord and growing from our mistakes.

THE CALL

During times of tribulation, God does not wish for us to run from Him. He wants us to run *to* Him. It is during these times that, we as human beings, grow in Christ. It is during these times we learn patience. We learn that we do not control our own destiny; that everything we thought we knew goes out the window. It is easy to become lost in this world and turn to worldly fixes. Take into account how Judas missed the true "being" of God. He was walking with the human version of God for three years and missed the call. We do not know if he had a lot of turmoil in his life, but we do know he caused turmoil by the choices he made. I'm not sure we will ever know if God's will for Judas' life was to miss his true calling. A countless number of people have missed God's calling in their lives. Those are the people that are currently and will be destined to spend eternity in Hell. The influence of those who have missed the call affects what happens on this earth, just as much as the folks that will spend eternity in Heaven. How do we, as human beings, truly live out the will God has for our lives?

In Philippians 3, Paul writes of his transformation from Pharisee to follower of Jesus. He discusses having "…no confidence in the flesh." In other words, having a lack of confidence in our humanly form. He lists all of the activities that once defined who he was before his transformation. He claims in verses 4–6 (NIV), "*[4] Though I myself have reasons for such confidence. If someone else thinks they have reasons to put confidence in the flesh, I have more: [5] circumcised on the eighth day, of the people of Israel, of the tribe of Benjamin, a Hebrew of Hebrews; in regard to the law, a Pharisee; [6] as for zeal, persecuting the church; as for righteousness based on the law, faultless.*"

He runs through what would have, in those days, made him very prestigious in society and would have given him great success in life. But as God's chosen, we must realize, as Solomon did in Ecclesiastes, that this world is only temporary. It is a moment in time in our existence, or for folks not a part of God's elite, part of their time of non-existence. If someone is destined for the lake of fire (aka Hell), and never decides to change to follow the will of God, while on this earth, then they, once dead in the flesh, will be dead in the spirit. Once dead in the spirit, and burning eternally in Hell, then they no longer have the opportunity to be a part of God's elite. They are and will be forever separated from God. Luke 16:19–31 (NIV) explains the parable of the Rich Man and Lazarus:

"19 There was a rich man who was dressed in purple and fine linen and lived in luxury every day. 20 At his gate was laid a beggar named Lazarus, covered with sores 21 and longing to eat what fell from the rich man's table. Even the dogs came and licked his sores.

"22 The time came when the beggar died and the angels carried him to Abraham's side. The rich man also died and was buried. 23 In Hades, where he was in torment, he looked up and saw Abraham far away, with Lazarus by his side. 24 So he called to him, 'Father Abraham, have pity on me and send Lazarus to dip the tip of his finger in water and cool my tongue, because I am in agony in this fire.'

"25 But Abraham replied, 'Son, remember that in your lifetime you received your good things, while Lazarus received bad things, but now he is comforted here and you are in agony. 26 And besides all this, between us and you a great chasm has been set in place, so that those who want to go from here to you cannot, nor can anyone cross over from there to us.'

"27 He answered, 'Then I beg you, father, send Lazarus to my family, 28 for I have five brothers. Let him warn them, so that they will not also come to this place of torment.'

"29 Abraham replied, 'They have Moses and the Prophets; let them listen to them.'

"30 No, father Abraham,' he said, 'but if someone from the dead goes to them, they will repent.'

"31 He said to him, 'If they do not listen to Moses and the Prophets, they will not be convinced even if someone rises from the dead.'"

Abraham basically tells the rich man that he missed his call in life. He spent his time being "rich" on Earth, rather than listening to the prophets before him and following their teachings. By the end of the parable, Abraham is so fed up with this guy's request that he exclaims that his family also has the same choice he did on Earth. We all have this choice on Earth. There will rarely be a miracle of someone being raised from the dead (or something like that) steering people towards God and His plan for their lives. Sometimes it is God's plan for those miracles to happen so someone will believe, but those are rare occasions.

Philippians 3:7 (NIV) explains how we should live our lives in regards to our earthly possessions. It reads, *"⁷ But whatever were gains to me I now consider loss for the sake of Christ."* After Paul tells the reader all of the things that would have made him a prestigious Jew of the day, he proceeds with his transformation in verse seven. Along the same lines of not letting your possessions control you, a way to discover your purpose in life is to (and this one is for all the millennials reading this), as Paul did, "delete" your fleshly desires.

We must humble ourselves in order to make room for God and the relationship He desires to have with us. Yes, that last line was for all the folks out there still with their egos intact. For me, my pride is a silly thing. Pride causes desire, and desire is a predecessor to some sins. Pride has been and will always be the downfall of mankind. Even as far back as Genesis, when Adam and Eve sinned in the Garden of Eden, our first ancestors were prideful. The Bible doesn't really explain whether or not they knew what pride was, but it was most likely a fairly new concept to them. God told them, in Genesis 2:16–17 (NIV), *"¹⁶ You are free to eat from any tree in the garden; ¹⁷ but you must not eat from the tree of the knowledge of good and evil, for when you eat from it you will certainly die."*

Like Adam and Eve, in modern days, Satan tricks us into believing that we can be like God if we would simply do one thing or another. By our fleshly nature, we take the bait and, let's be honest, do stupid things that we know better not to do. We so easily lose sight of what God has planned for our lives. Like Paul, and many other examples in the Bible, humbling oneself is part of submitting to the will of God. In Luke 23:32–43 (NIV), we learn of a man who is known to us as the reader, as a criminal:

"³² Two other men, both criminals, were also led out with him to be executed. ³³ When they came to the place called the Skull, they crucified him there, along with the criminals—one on his right, the other on his left. ³⁴ Jesus said, 'Father, forgive them, for they do not know what they are doing.' And they divided up his clothes by casting lots. ³⁵ The people stood watching, and the rulers even sneered at him. They said, 'He saved others; let him save himself if he is God's Messiah, the Chosen One.' ³⁶ The soldiers also came up and mocked him. They offered him wine vinegar ³⁷ and said, 'If you are the king of the Jews, save yourself.' ³⁸ There was a written notice above him, which read: THIS IS THE KING OF THE JEWS. ³⁹ One of the criminals who hung there hurled insults at him: 'Aren't you the Messiah? Save yourself and us!' ⁴⁰ But the other criminal rebuked him. 'Don't you fear God,' he said, 'since you are under the same sentence? ⁴¹ We are punished justly, for we are getting what our deeds deserve. But this man has done nothing wrong.' Then he said, 'Jesus, remember me when you come into your kingdom.' ⁴³ Jesus answered him, 'Truly I tell you, today you will be with me in paradise.'"

If we can just say—and I know this isn't easy for us to do all the time—"God, please forgive me, for I am a sinner," we would walk around more often feeling forgiven. In feeling forgiven, we could feel more confident that God is walking with us. In feeling more confident that God is walking with us, as God's chosen, just imagine what that could bring to our society. Submission of oneself is a step to knowing the will of God.

If you have not discovered this on your own, I hate to be the first to break it to you, but as much as we think we are in control, we are simply not. Whether you believe in God or not, life has a way of simply happening. You can control bits and pieces of it, but in the grand scheme of things, it's not possible. You can try to hold on to it as long as you can, but in the end, you lose it whether you want to or not. Like any good mental health program, the first step is acknowledgment. In this case, it is the acknowledgment that you do not have control over your life. You don't even have control over the next breath you take.

In Philippians 1, Paul is writing to the church in Philippi from prison, where he was bound in chains for preaching God's word. Paul is questioning life or death, but all the while, he is proclaiming life is a choice. He finds reason for his life; he realizes his purpose is not for himself, but for others. Paul, of course, shows throughout scripture that he was willing and did submit himself to Christ and the life God planned for him. Philippians 1:18–26 (NIV) reads:

"[18] But what does it matter? The important thing is that in every way, whether from false motives or true, Christ is preached. And because of this I rejoice. Yes, and I will continue to rejoice, [19] for I know that through your prayers and God's provision of the Spirit of Jesus Christ what has happened to me will turn out for my deliverance [20] I eagerly expect and hope that I will in no way be ashamed, but will have sufficient courage so that now as always Christ will be exalted in my body, whether by life or by death. [21] For to me, to live is Christ and to die is gain. [22] If I am to go on living in the body, this will mean fruitful labor for me. Yet what shall I choose? I do not know! [23] I am torn between the two: I desire to depart and be with Christ, which is better by far; [24] but it is more necessary for you that I remain in the body. [25] Convinced of this, I know that I will remain, and I will continue with all of you for your progress and joy in the faith, [26] so that through my being with you again your boasting in Christ Jesus will abound on account of me."

There is a choice we all make on a daily basis if one believes in God. Will I follow God, or will I not? Your actions answer that question. Your thoughts answer that question. The people that you let affect your life answer that question. Why not let God answer that question for you through His word? He has answered it for you; will you submit and accept it? If a person is willing to submit to the will of God, they will be part of His chosen few. They are always welcome to be a part of God's family. You are always able to be a part of God's family.

Submission to not only reading but following God's word is how God's chosen live their lives. If you think to yourself, *well, I go to church every Sunday, I read my Bible daily, I pray every morning, and do a devotion; I am definitely one of God's chosen people*, then check yourself! As we learn in Matthew 4:1–11 (NIV), even Satan knows the scripture: *"¹ Then Jesus was led by the Spirit into the wilderness to be tempted by the devil. ² After fasting forty days and forty nights, he was hungry. ³ The tempter came to him and said, 'If you are the Son of God, tell these stones to become bread.' ⁴ Jesus answered, 'It is written: "Man shall not live on bread alone, but on every word that comes from the mouth of God."' ⁵ Then the devil took him to the holy city and had him stand on the highest point of the temple. ⁶ 'If you are the Son of God,' he said, 'throw yourself down. For it is written: "He will command his angels concerning you, and they will lift you up in their hands, so that you will not strike your foot against a stone."' ⁷ Jesus answered him, 'It is also written: "Do not put the Lord your God to the test."' ⁸ Again, the devil took him to a very high mountain and showed him all the kingdoms of the world and their splendor. ⁹ 'All this I will give you,' he said, 'if you will bow down and worship me.' ¹⁰ Jesus said to him, 'Away from me, Satan! For it is written: "Worship the Lord your God, and serve him only."' ¹¹ Then the devil left him, and angels came and attended him"*

Complete surrender. A relationship with you is what God longs for. His love for us is unfailing and can only be overcome by our inability, or the lack of desire, to accept it. There is a phase in the process of submission where an individual must surrender something. In this case, it's not compromising. It is complete and utter surrender. It's God's way or the highway. The Bible tells us, *"Don't copy the behavior and customs of this world, but let God transform you into a new person by changing the way you think. Then you will learn to know God's will for you, which is good and pleasing and perfect" (Romans 12:2 NLT).*

You have to ask yourself, "What are my true motives and/or intentions?" God does not want a religious fiend taking part in His kingdom. In the New Testament, Jesus is always quarreling with the religious scholars of the day. On many occasions, He makes them look like fools in public. Enough so, that in the end, they killed Him. All part of God's plan, yes. God does not want us to be religious drones.

What does submission look like? It all comes down to love and showing God's love to and serving others wholeheartedly. I'm giving you the answer upfront on this one. I'm going to be honest with you all; love has been a struggle of mine for the greater part of my life. One of the greatest difficulties in this life is to love someone who persecutes you. We learn this message in Matthew 5 when Jesus tells us: *"[43] You have heard that it was said, 'Love your neighbor and hate your enemy.' [44] But I tell you, love your enemies and pray for those who persecute you, [45] that you may be children of your Father in heaven. He causes his sun to rise on the evil and the good, and sends rain on the righteous and the unrighteous. [46] If you love those who love you, what reward will you get? Are not even the tax collectors doing that? [47] And if you greet only your own people, what are you doing more than others? Do not even pagans do that? [48] Be perfect, therefore, as your heavenly Father is perfect"* (Matthew 5:43-48 NIV)

Everyone in this world has been hurt by someone else in this world. Unfortunately, this is a simple fact of life: hurt is caused by sin. We have to look at how God responds to sin. God forgives the sins of those who ask. What if the person that hurt you doesn't ask for forgiveness? Then what? God loves everyone on this planet, even when they do not respond to Him. Just remember, Jesus was beaten and eventually hung on a cross by the same people He loved. In one of His final breaths, He forgave them.

Forgiveness not only of others but of oneself. In some cases, forgiving yourself for what you have done is the most important thing you can do and is the only key to unlocking your freedom from sin. Remove yourself to make room for God. The scope of this is massive. This touches on removing anything from our lives that is ungodly or is getting in the way of us following God. This could be a person, a thing, a place, you name it (place a noun here). Humans have the ability to make anything a god, even ourselves. Remove yourself. Seek God.

In 2 Corinthians 12: 1–10 (NIV), Paul tells us that sometimes God allows weakness in our lives in order for Him to shine through. Sometimes in this life, we can get a little conceited. Based on this scripture, I submit to you that Paul's old self (Saul) would come out every once in awhile, and he may have gotten a little cocky. So God stepped in... *"1 I must go on boasting. Although there is nothing to be gained, I will go on to visions and revelations from the Lord. 2 **I know a man in Christ who fourteen years ago was caught up to the third heaven. Whether it was in the body or out of the body I do not know—God knows. 3 And I know that this man—whether in the body or apart from the body I do not know, but God knows—4 was caught up to paradise and heard inexpressible things, things that no one is permitted to tell. 5 I will boast about a man like that, but I will not boast about myself, except about my weaknesses.** 6 Even if I should choose to boast, I would not be a fool, because I would be speaking the truth. But I refrain, so no one will think more of me than is warranted by what I do or say, 7 **or because of these surpassingly great revelations. Therefore, in order to keep me from becoming conceited, I was given a thorn in my flesh, a messenger of Satan, to torment me. 8 Three times I pleaded with the Lord to take it away from me.** 9 But he said to me, "My grace is sufficient for you, for my power is made perfect in weakness." Therefore I will boast all the more gladly about my weaknesses, so that Christ's power may rest on me. 10 **That is why, for Christ's sake, I delight in weaknesses, in insults, in hardships, in persecutions, in difficulties. For when I am weak, then I am strong."*

If you are like Paul and have a thorn in your side or something that is a burden you cannot overcome on your own, take it to God the Father. He, and only He, has the power to take it away if it is His will for your life. How do we know if our struggles are caused by our sin or if it is something God wants us to face? To figure this out, you must commit to something very simple (it's actually very difficult): Examine your heart.

How often do you examine yourself? Once a day? Once a minute? Every few seconds? Do you ever examine your thoughts and intentions? In living in this world for 30-something years, I would submit to you that there is a wide range of self-examination on society's scale. You have the extremists who believe they must always be conscious of who they are, and you have the easy-going type of person that goes with the flow. Each person has a purpose in God's eyes, so if you are one or the other, don't worry—God's plan is different for each of you. Maybe being extreme on either end is practical, but in my life, I have found that examining myself routinely helps clarify my true intentions. Of course, I'm not perfect, but I have tried to live my life with God's purpose always in the back of my mind, examining my heart and trying to align the two. I would encourage you wholeheartedly to do the same. Whether you examine yourself once a day or once a month, just keep at it, and God will show you what He has for you in this life. The Bible encourages us to examine ourselves in 1 Corinthians 11:28 before taking the element of communion.

For those of you who do not know what communion is, don't worry, and please don't feel discouraged. This is the simple practice of eating bread (typically unleavened) and juice (throughout history, it used to be wine, now it is grape juice), symbolizing the acceptance of Jesus' body and blood that was sacrificed for our sins. In the new testament, Jesus first gives communion to His disciples at the last supper, in which He tells them "to do this in remembrance of me" (referring to taking communion).

1 Corinthians 11:23–29 (NIV) tells us, *"²³ For I received from the Lord what I also passed on to you: The Lord Jesus, on the night he was betrayed, took bread, ²⁴ and when he had given thanks, he broke it and said, 'This is my body, which is for you; do this in remembrance of me.' ²⁵ In the same way, after supper he took the cup, saying, 'This cup is the new covenant in my blood; do this, whenever you drink it, in remembrance of me.' ²⁶ For whenever you eat this bread and drink this cup, you proclaim the Lord's death until he comes. ²⁷ So then, whoever eats the bread or drinks the cup of the Lord in an unworthy manner will be guilty of sinning against the body and blood of the Lord. ²⁸ Everyone ought to examine themselves before they eat of the bread and drink from the cup. ²⁹ For those who*

eat and drink without discerning the body of Christ eat and drink judgment on themselves."

Communion gives us a sense of renewal within our spiritual journey in life. In some cases, it has been ritualized, but in its true meaning it is a covenant with God, telling Him that with the physical elements, one is committing to follow the teachings of Jesus and to live in love. To get to this place, one must do a few things prior to taking the elements.

As we have been through already, "examine your heart." In this world, you may have heard sayings such as "just follow your heart" or "home is where the heart is." Examining one's heart is not about the fluffy statements of the world. It is a serious time of self-reflection in which one examines a list of rights and wrongs that he or she has committed. The good news is Jesus takes the wrongs away if they ask Him. During times of self-reflection and communion the person is telling God, yes, I have sinned, and I own it. The assumption is that that person also asks for forgiveness in the same regard. Another reason to examine one's heart is so that an individual accounts for themself. Romans 2:5–7 (ESV) says, *"⁵ But because of your hard and unrepentant heart, you are storing up wrath against yourself for the day of wrath, when God's righteous judgment will be revealed. ⁶ God 'will repay each one according to his deeds.' ⁷ To those who by perseverance in doing good seek glory, honor, and immortality, He will give eternal life…"*

Without the examining portion of your life, not only in communion but examination as a whole, how would one know what "deeds" they have done? The answer is they wouldn't realize the "deeds." They would live this life as if there were no consequences, falling into the same traps over and over again. Committing the same sins over and over again. Sound familiar? I know I can look back at my life and see the times where I had more time for reflection and the times I did not. I can attest there is freedom and change when self-reflection occurs. This is, in part, how we grow in our faith and as human beings.

Another way one must examine himself or herself is by examining his or her thought process. Simply put, think about how you think. This will assist in giving you the self-discipline to fulfill God's plan for your life. In knowing one's thought process, a person can think a little bit deeper on the *why* of whatever life throws their way. For example, if you're a little OCD like me, even minor changes in life can be difficult. I like things in a particular order. I have grown through Christ over the years and now when change does come, I can manage it easier than what I could even four or five years ago. Through self-reflection and prayer, God has helped me learn about myself and how to maintain composure in the midst of stress.

Likewise, examining our heart helps us learn what drives us. What are you driven by? Is it positive or negative? Take a minute and look deep inside yourself. What are you allowing to motivate your life? Being driven is not only feelings-based or thoughts-based. Being driven is looking at something in this world, and/or the next, and realizing that this thing controls how you operate. It feeds your life and your life's habits. As God has given us the freedom to choose, we can choose whether or not to be driven by positive or negative things. (Please keep in mind that motive can also be action-based.) I encourage you to show your true self to…well, yourself. Stop lying to yourself and pretending that everything is okay. In some cases it may be, but we all have faults at every point in life. We all have struggles that control us. If you know how you feel about things (what your heart wants), you know how you think about things (knowing your thought process), and you know what motivates you (how you are driven), you can and will grow as an individual. It takes time, and we all have to learn patience, but growth and maturity will come. When it does, you and I will be better for it. Our society will be better for it. Love will be better for it because that gets us to the purest source of love—God.

If you want the perfect way not to examine yourself, take a look at Judas. In the Bible, there is not really any note of Judas reflecting upon how he is reacting to things. There are a few references to him scheming (i.e., Luke 22:4) with the chief priests to execute Jesus. Also, he must have done some sort of self-reflection before he hanged himself after betraying Jesus. Regardless, not the best example of good self-reflection methods practiced by Judas.

Take Paul, on the other hand. Good self-reflection practices. He wrote two-thirds of the New Testament. I think it's obvious how he practiced his self-reflection skills. He basically set the bar on self-reflection. I mean, of course, there were others before him, such as many of the Old Testament characters in the Bible, but he paved the way on how to act, post Jesus' death and resurrection. As strong as Paul was in following God's will for his life, he still struggled. As it was, he had something he couldn't get rid of. Something that dug into him. Something that drove his decisions in life, to some extent. Something negative as he asked God to take it away from him. This world threw a lot at Paul, but yet he was successful in completing the mission God had for his life.

ADDICTION

The *Merriam-Webster Dictionary* defines the term "addiction" as "a compulsive, chronic, physiological or psychological need for a habit-forming substance, behavior, or activity having harmful physical, psychological, or social effects and typically causing well-defined symptoms (such as anxiety, irritability, tremors, or nausea) upon withdrawal or abstinence : the state of being addicted."

It is a term modern-day society uses when they don't know how to describe a stronghold of sin. In biblical times, it seems that they would use terms like "a thorn in my flesh, a messenger of Satan, to torment me," as Paul refers to it. With that said, Paul may not be describing something that was truly, in modern terms, an addiction, but the comparison here comes in terms of his weakness. Simply put, addiction is a human weakness—weakness that can only be describes with words like "trauma" and "torment." When it comes to addiction, in this day and age, we use terms like "severe trauma" to describe the outcome of the act known as an addiction. Paul uses the term "torment." Paul has defined his addiction with a term that alludes to there being a spiritual aspect to addiction. That, and the fact that he calls his addiction a "messenger of Satan." Just think about it for a second. Next time you are talking with someone about an issue you have or an addiction, just say, "this is a messenger of Satan" and see what kind of reaction you get. People will most likely look at you sideways.

Anyway, the point is, by today's standards, the definition of addiction and how society sees it is non-spiritual ("psychologically or physically"), rather than in the old days, when it was based on Satan and/or his messengers. As such, can we go ahead and all agree that someone can be predestined to be addicted? Paul determined that his addiction was given to him for a purpose. ("Therefore, in order to keep me from becoming conceited, I was given a thorn in my flesh.") And in verses 8 and 9 of 2 Corinthians 12 (NIV), Paul continues, "*8 Three times I pleaded with the Lord to take it away from me. 9 But he said to me, 'My grace is sufficient for you, for my power is made perfect in weakness.'*"

Paul describes his issue as being "given" to him. And when Paul spoke with God about it, God said it was given to Paul because His "power is made perfect in weakness." Mind blown… God's power is made perfect through our weaknesses? What? Think about it this way—God has no weakness. He understands completely what weakness is and how it works. Weakness is one thing that keeps us, as humans, from becoming God. I equate this to something today called a "reality check." Why did Paul receive his "thorn?" It was to relinquish him of his own pride, so he did not think of himself too highly. God allows us to have weaknesses so that through them, He can make us stronger and shape us through maturity. Weakness is the mechanism by which we grow spiritually, mentally, and even physically. In our walk with Christ, there has to be a testament to His power and His grace. Without a testament, there is no need for God. There is only a need for "self."

The key takeaway to 2 Corinthians 12 is that Paul continues to walk with God even with the "thorn in his flesh." No matter what addiction(s) you may have, you can still walk with God through that. Think of the most jacked, most ripped person you know. Then think of the skinniest, least fit type of person you know. Who is more likely to influence someone off the street to go to the gym? The jacked person, of course. See, physical muscle is like spiritual muscle. Physical muscle is built by working out, by "gettin' your fitness on." Your muscles actually tear when you work out, but not to the extent of tearing so badly you have long term pain after every workout. But when one is done with a workout, they can feel the soreness over the following days until those muscles heal and become stronger. If one continues to work out routinely, they get jacked, or at least in better physical shape than what they were before working out. The buff people (fitness experts) of this world are those who get everyone else to go to the gym, not only because they look good, but because they are healthy. Just as working out can help your physical muscle grow, your weaknesses can help your spiritual muscles grow. With that said, God does not call us to dwell on sin. If we focus too hard on overcoming the sin, sometimes that makes it more difficult to overcome. Giving it up to God is the only way to get rid of sin.

As intentions and motives are what drive our choices, the Bible guides us in making better choices. The Bible is the ultimate guide to life for God's children. It spells out what your intentions and motives should be when guided by the Holy Spirit. It explains how our actions lead us one way or another (i.e., submission to God's plan for our lives always provides a good outcome in life). It also gives us guidance on what it means to walk by the spirit.

I ask you to consider that your intentions should always be to walk by the spirit, to grow in the spirit, and to love the way God loves. Galatians 5:13–21 (NIV) explains how we should live in our freedom: *"13 You, my brothers and sisters, were called to be free. But do not use your freedom to indulge the flesh; rather, serve one another humbly in love. 14 For the entire law is fulfilled in keeping this one command: 'Love your neighbor as yourself.' 15 If you bite and devour each other, watch out or you will be destroyed by each other. 16 So I say, walk by the Spirit, and you will not gratify the desires of the flesh. [17] For the flesh desires what is contrary to the Spirit, and the Spirit what is contrary to the flesh. They are in conflict with each other, so that you are not to do whatever you want. [18] But if you are led by the Spirit, you are not under the law. [19] The acts of the flesh are obvious: sexual immorality, impurity and debauchery; [20] idolatry and witchcraft; hatred, discord, jealousy, fits of rage, selfish ambition, dissensions, factions [21] and envy; drunkenness, orgies, and the like. I warn you, as I did before, that those who live like this will not inherit the kingdom of God."*

There is a fine line between addiction and just making bad choices over and over again. The issues you may have are between you and God. Sometimes addiction needs to be talked about with other people. If there is a thorn in your flesh, and you can know that you're not alone, pray and seek God, even if you feel unworthy. He will guide your path on how to handle things. You may be like Paul. He may not take it away, so one day, he can use it for His good.

In Mark 14:32–42, we see another example of how God does not take away a situation that Jesus asks Him to take away. In this account, we see the human side of Jesus. This is the last piece of scripture in Mark that is given before Jesus is arrested. Jesus and the disciples are in the garden of Gethsemane, praying before Jesus is taken away to be crucified. Of course, at the time, Jesus knew what was going to happen, but the disciples may not have known the full story of what was to come. Jesus tells them to stay in one spot and "keep watch." The Bible doesn't tell us what they were watching for, but they were supposed to be looking for something (probably the people coming to arrest Jesus). They fall asleep three times, and each time, Jesus is frustrated about it. Regardless of the disciples sleeping, not praying or keeping watch, Jesus prays to God while he is alone saying (verse 36 NIV), *"And he said, 'Abba, Father, all things are possible for you. Remove this cup from me. Yet not what I will, but what you will.'"* We all know the end of the story, Jesus is crucified and dies and rises again. Now He is in Heaven sitting at the right hand of the Father. This is not an account of addiction but an account of having an immense event that Jesus had to overcome as a human. He (the Son of God) even pleading with God to ask if there was another way, take it from Him. Sometimes the pain of this world is necessary for God's plan to be complete; it was even the case for Jesus, His son.

Jesus was not an addict, but He became sin so that sin may be put to death on the cross. Paul may or may not have had some sort of addiction, but he had a thorn by which some sort of continuous sin or human discomfort had a level of control over his life. These two men were godly men. Jesus was, of course, God himself, but Paul was one of the most famous prophets ever to walk this earth. Though they ask God to take away their burdens that weighed heavy on their lives, and God did not take their burdens away, they still stayed true to God and His plan for their lives. They withheld their faith and, in turn, carried out an example of spiritual discipline we can focus on even in today's time.

DISCIPLINE

As followers of Christ, we must acknowledge that we have a calling in our lives to understand authority and submit to authority. The concept of obeying/submitting to authority is something we all must learn over and over again throughout our lives. It is a daily battle of will to let God have authority over your life. If God does not have authority over your life, then what does? I can guarantee you that it is something of this world, or not of this world, that opposes our Heavenly Father. God does not like to be put second. He will allow you to put Him second in this life, but that doesn't always turn out well for people in the end (hint, hint…they end up in Hell for eternity).

When we look at Judas and Paul, we can see that Judas lacked discipline in his life, while Paul, once he identified himself as Saul, succeeded in discipline. Paul writes of spiritual discipline in Galatians 5. Yes, one of the more read chapters in the Bible, also known for listing the fruits of the spirit. The fruits of the spirit are simply notes on how a Christ follower can remain disciplined in the faith. Agreeing with yourself to follow these guidelines, Paul (interceding for God) has given us the easiest way to love your neighbors. Paul humbled himself on the road to Damascus by following God's instruction. We will not always have a clear instruction from God. This world causes us to consider and reconsider everything in it and about it. Then all of a sudden, we potentially become lost. Paul, among many others we can refer to in the Bible, lived out his faith in Christ. Not always perfectly, but they were all human beings just like we are.

I encourage you to read Galatians 5 in its entirety. But for this message, please consider Galatians 5:1 (NIV), *"It is for freedom that Christ has set us free. Stand firm, then, and do not let yourselves be burdened again by a yoke of slavery."* And Galatians 5:13–14 (NIV), *"¹³ You, my brothers and sisters, were called to be free. But do not use your freedom to indulge the flesh; rather, serve one another humbly in love. ¹⁴ For the entire law is fulfilled in keeping this one command: 'Love your neighbor as yourself.'"*

I give you this thought to ponder: Is loving God and loving your neighbors in the way that the Bible explains in Galatians 5 and other passages committing us to the act of spiritual discipline? I believe we can all agree that the answer is a resounding "yes!" Paul declares that we are already free once we accept Christ as our Lord and Savior. God gives us the guidelines to truly gain our freedom from this world, throughout the Bible, from what we can't understand, and from Satan and his attacks on our lives. We just have to keep pushing forward, keep moving forward through life, by God's means, and by God's strength. Not our own.

DISTRACTIONS

So why is it so hard to put all of this into practice and live for Christ? Why is it so difficult to practice self-discipline? The simple answer is distractions. Have you ever been distracted by something? Have you ever thought of something for a long time? Something that, in the end, didn't even matter? Something that made you lose focus on the things that do matter or did matter at the time? I don't know about you, but this happens to me all the time. It happens most often in my prayer life. Taking you back really quick to Matthew 4. Verses 2–3 tell us that Jesus was tempted by the devil after fasting for 40 days and nights, and he was hungry. I will say the most I am distracted is when I am tired and hungry. All I can think about is *how do I get food?* or *how do I find the nearest bed to sleep in?* Jesus, in Matthew 4, was being tempted by the devil. There is a distinct feature of being distracted versus being tempted. In being tempted, there is an implication of potential sin, whereas being distracted is not always carried by our sinful nature. Simply put, we can act on a distraction without committing a sin, but if we act on a temptation, then we commit a sin.

Take death or a life-threatening illness, for instance. This could be a family member, a friend, or someone you barely knew; it could be a human being, a pet, or some other entity that had the capability to love. Whatever or whoever it is or was, the loss of love is the hardest distraction in life. We still don't completely understand why illness and/or death happens when it does. Growing up, my pastor's son, Darrell Jr., was a fit person. He played all types of sports. He was active in the church and in the community. One day, he was playing a pick-up game of basketball and passed out unexpectedly on the court and died. I'm not quite sure if they ever found a diagnosis or not, but the last I had heard, they never did. Darrell Jr. stood up for me growing up. When the 5'5", skinnier, non-muscular version of me would cower to aggression, his 6'4", 250-pound stature would "carry some weight," so to speak. He was a good friend, and he would be there for people. I loved him as a brother.

Likewise, Natalie and I had a long-haired Dachshund named Molly. Molly had just turned 12 years old. She was the happiest and most calm dog I had ever met, and my wife and I loved her. She was loyal and had a personality, comparative to a human. She was sassy, kind, loving, and was always looking for a treat. She was always there for Natalie and me when we needed someone. She was our good friend and, in a sense, kind of like our first child. But one day, shortly after she turned 12 years old, Molly was not acting like herself. She wasn't eating (which was a huge sign something was wrong), and she was limping. She had had some hip and back issues, as most Dachshunds do at that age. We took her to the vet, and we came to find out it was a tumor in her heart. It was one of the most aggressive tumors out there, and the vet gave her a few days to live. She said it would not be a pretty few days, so that next afternoon, we had to put Molly down. I'm not sure if dogs have a soul or not, but in interacting with Molly for six years of my life, I could tell she cared for Natalie and me. She had some sense of emotion, whether it was replicated/mimicked or not. She was with us for a time; she had life. Then life was taken from her. It made Natalie and me very sad. She was a good friend to us, human or not. She brought us joy and love in our lives. I loved her as a daughter.

When someone we love suddenly passes on to the next life, their love leaves too. It is not easy for the people left here on Earth. It's hard to make sense of the loss of love. We simply tend to the question of "Why do good people/pets die?" Why does life leave? The living has the pain of those that have left, in some cases, with no sense of if they went to Heaven or Hell. We simply do not know. The hardest part of loss is the void of not having that person's love in our lives. Sometimes our mourning can be the hardest distraction to overcome. Love is the hardest thing to suppress and get over. I'm not sure we ever stop loving someone we have truly loved. When they are gone, we love what those entities used to be; how we knew them when they were alive. If we are not careful, sometimes that can keep us from moving forward. It is human nature to have a season of mourning and pain, but the distraction comes when we stay in the season for too long. Mourning is a healthy emotion, but it was not intended to be long term. We must leave even the hardest distraction—loss of love—when the time is right. God can relinquish that pain.

In this day and age, we have developed many other ways to become distracted. We have mini-computers in our pockets/purses at all times. We can order something online and have it delivered to our front door within the hour. We can look up sports scores, the stock market, the latest clothing fad, the latest viral video, etc., at any given moment. When my wife and I are out on our dates or just having dinner out at a restaurant, we always notice the people who are on their cell phones. One evening, we were at dinner with some friends, and we noticed a table of about 10 to 15 high-school-aged persons who were dressed up and looked like they were going to dinner before a school dance. Not one was talking to the person next to them or across the table from them, at least from what we could see. They all had their heads down, looking at their phones. If it has not become the struggle already, this will be the struggle of the next generation;—cell phone/information technology use.

This particular example of technology usage is not necessarily usage of a sinful nature. Let's be honest, "checking in" on Facebook is not a sin (for the most part). It's probably not the smartest thing to do from a life security standpoint, but most likely, it's not a sin. The question you have to ask yourself, in not only the instances of "checking in" on Facebook but in every circumstance you encounter, is "does this 'thing' that I'm doing bring glory to God?" Before there were cell phones (and I know we all remember that time, except for some of the millennial generation), folks were still distracted by the things of this world. It was not the information technology age back then, but there were still plenty of things to be distracted by. The Bible gives us a story about this in Luke 10:

"*38 As Jesus and his disciples were on their way, he came to a village where a woman named Martha opened her home to him. 39 She had a sister called Mary, who sat at the Lord's feet listening to what he said. 40 But Martha was distracted by all the preparations that had to be made. She came to him and asked, 'Lord, don't you care that my sister has left me to do the work by myself? Tell her to help me!' 41 'Martha, Martha,' the Lord answered, 'you are worried and upset about many things, 42 but few things are needed—or indeed only one. Mary has chosen what is better, and it will not be taken away from her'"* (Luke 10:38–42 NIV).

One could be distracted by anything in this world. It could be too much time on the computer/television. It could be your past. Distractions don't always come in the form of a physical element. Many folks in this world can't get over their pasts. This is why we have people in this world that study human behavior and societal behavior. Not saying, in all cases, that people in general can't alleviate themselves from their past, but it is truly something that some people struggle with. I'm going to let you in on a little secret: You and I can't change the past.

Even Paul had regrets. He had thoughts he felt were God's will, but it turned out, God allowed Satan to block Paul. Yes, it turns out, Satan can block us. Oh, boy! Something else to worry about. Just kidding. Don't worry about it; God's got your back. Paul wrote in 1 Thessalonians 2:17–18 (NIV):

"17 But, brothers and sisters, when we were orphaned by being separated from you for a short time (in person, not in thought), out of our intense longing we made every effort to see you. 18 For we wanted to come to you—certainly I, Paul, did, again and again—but Satan blocked our way."

Paul had a deep yearning to see the ones he loved in this region. Yet, it just never worked out. If you ever long to see someone you love who lives far away, just remember, Satan might be blocking you from seeing them, or in life's challenges/distractions, the obstacles of life aren't allowing you to see them. Either way you would like to look at it, life is hard when you can't see loved ones when you want to. Regardless of where life takes you or where Satan blocks you, don't live in regret. God will bring you through, and if it works out, then it is His will that you see your loved ones. If you dwell on regrets or on your past, Satan has a grasp on you from moving forward in your growth in your spiritual walk with the Holy Spirit.

In being a Christ follower from such a young age, I had to learn not to dwell in the past. My distraction in life was my past. I could not pull myself out of it. Today, I look at my life through a new lens. This lens can only be from God. My past is no longer an issue. There have been a couple of tools that God has given me to overcome the temptation to dwell on my past. First, God has given me a beautiful wife and family to hold on to. I couldn't tell you what day it was, but there was a day when I realized I needed to be an example for my family. I needed to be there to support them and love them through all of life's circumstances. I needed, and need to be, today and every day, the loving husband and father God has called me to be. God will give you something to hold on to. It may not be a family of your own. It will be something fitting to your path in life.

Second, God gave me a purpose to serve. My wife, Natalie, and I began praying for our purpose together once we got married. She and I are very alike in this manner; we always wants to know the "why" of the situation. So we often ask ourselves, "Why are we here?" and "What is our purpose for being here?" No matter where we have been in life, where we are now, or where God is taking us, we always wonder what the next step is in life. I can tell you that God uses the little things in life to provide you with purpose. I am always looking for the next big thing. Human nature tells us to "go big or go home." This world tells us you can have anything your heart desires. God tells us to "ask and we shall receive… according to His purpose or plan." I have had to humble myself on this one. I always want to have God's plan be something so extravagant that it leaves my name in history. I can tell you from experience, 99 times out of 100, this is not the case. Service, in God's will, accounts for all the little things in life. I relate this to Sunday School teaching. My wife and I have taught a variety of ages of Sunday School classes. In reality, kids are rambunctious and energetic; most of them don't like to sit still, and they all have an opinion these days. Regardless, even though Sunday after Sunday, we feel we are not getting through to them with the concepts and teachings of the Bible, we are. My purpose of serving in the church we attend is part of God's plan for my life.

Third, God has given me purpose in simply talking to Him. Prayer, though at times seems so simple (or difficult, depending on the day), has given me purpose. Talking to God as my Heavenly

Father, my friend, and someone I can lean on has been extremely important in my everyday life. I can honestly tell you, on the days that it seems like I have no time to pray, I feel differently (more anxious, angrier, less loving, etc.) than on days it seems I do have time to pray. Prayer is very important in your walk with God.

Along with prayer, purpose comes when you start training your mind to control your thoughts. Many times, we don't realize it until it happens, but our minds go awry, and we think of ungodly things. God wants us to give our thoughts to Him. He desires to be the center of our lives. The Devil easily manipulates our thoughts and desires. Part of our everyday prayer needs to be, "God, please give me strength to control my thoughts... I give my thoughts to you." How you think is how you act. If you think bad thoughts, you're going to act grumpy, and no one likes a grumpy person.

In manipulating the truth, Satan can easily distract you. All it takes is sin. As sin is the ultimate distraction. It can cause us to doubt the truth. It causes us to doubt our ability to fulfill God's plan for our lives. Sin is simply committing an act, thought, or desire that does not follow the laws God has put in place. Oftentimes, we are committing sins and do not even know it. This is why we must take time to pray and ask God to direct our paths. This is the only way to defeat Satan's attempt to have us fall into temptation. We must have a commitment to God, our Father to avoid falling into the temptation of this world.

COMMITMENT

Something that Judas lacked that other characters in the Bible, such as Paul, did not, is a true commitment to God and the Lord, Jesus Christ. The final piece of being God's chosen is the commitment to the cause. The true commitment of laying down your life to God's plan. Jesus gives an example of what true commitment was for one man in Matthew 19:16–24 (NIV):

"*[16] Just then a man came up to Jesus and asked, 'Teacher, what good thing must I do to get eternal life?' [17] 'Why do you ask me about what is good?' Jesus replied. 'There is only One who is good. If you want to enter life, keep the commandments.'* [18] *'Which ones?' he inquired. Jesus replied, 'You shall not murder, you shall not commit adultery, you shall not steal, you shall not give false testimony,* [19] *honor your father and mother, and "love your neighbor as yourself."'* [20] *'All these I have kept,' the young man said. 'What do I still lack?'* [21] *Jesus answered, 'If you want to be perfect, go, sell your possessions and give to the poor, and you will have treasure in heaven. Then come, follow me.'* [22] *When the young man heard this, he went away sad, because he had great wealth.* [23] *Then Jesus said to his disciples, 'Truly I tell you, it is hard for someone who is rich to enter the kingdom of heaven.* [24] *Again I tell you, it is easier for a camel to go through the eye of a needle than for someone who is rich to enter the kingdom of God.'"*

Now, before you go off and sell everything you own and give it to the poor, genuinely ask yourself (and, of course, pray a lot about it): "Is this what God has called me to do?" Here's the thing. God calls each of us in different ways. Sometimes we are called to do the exact same thing as others, but sometimes we are called to "go it alone." Regardless of what your calling is, always, always, always seek God on the matter, and He will direct your path. The man in the parable was unable to freely choose God's will for his life. The passage tells us he struggled with the fact that all his possessions had to be given up. I think the question you have to ask yourself is, "Could I do it?" Could you give up everything you own to follow God? Fortunately, God does not want us all to live in poverty, so after reading this passage, you can rest assured that He does not call us all to give everything we have away. The real message here is not to be obsessed with your possessions. God wants our entire heart. He doesn't want to be second to anything, or anyone. I have always used this parable as a gauge for humbling myself in life. The question I ask myself is, "How much do I love this world and the things of it?" When, or if, you ever ask yourself this question, don't ponder on it too long, because you get into things of giving up your loved ones and the sort.

In the Old Testament, there is a book of the Bible called "Job." Job (the man) loved God. God had blessed Job and his family because of Job's loyalty to God and the love he had for God. In a nutshell, God allowed Satan to tempt Job and to test his faith. This included things like causing his livestock to die off, allowing his family to die off, and personal illness. In the end, Job overcame the tests and trials of the Devil and stayed true to God's will for his life. Now, he is an example of how we should follow God. Job's faith was one of the strongest ever recorded. I have faced trials of sorts in my life, but nothing that catastrophic, and my faith was nowhere close to what Job's was. Well, what about those times in the later chapters of Job when Job begins to deny God's posture? I submit to you that many of us would not last that long before making those claims. But that, of course, is when God steps into the story and corrects Job before he goes off the deep end. His faith was strong through the most terrible of times.

Like Paul, Job was committed to God's will. By the end of his story, he knew what was best for his life, and that was trusting God. By the end of his story, any doubt he had about God walking with him through his trials was overcome. Job's story ends with God blessing him and giving him two-fold of everything he owned, including a new family. God gives us the passage of Job to bring us hope; to encourage us to do His will in our lives. These types of messages strengthen our faith that God is who He says He is. They tell us, "It's okay to take a leap of faith because I (God) have come through for others in the past." It shows us God's faithful track record for those who love Him. If we are committed to God's will, hope comes naturally. Trust comes naturally. Faith comes naturally. If we CHOSE to be God's CHOSEN, then God will remain with us through all of life's trials and tribulations. He will never leave us nor forsake us.

7

THE LAST CHAPTER

Returning the focus to Ecclesiastes 3, in verses 9–14 (NIV), Solomon writes, *"⁹ What do workers gain from their toil? ¹⁰ I have seen the burden God has laid on the human race. ¹¹ He has made everything beautiful in its time. He has also set eternity in the human heart; yet no one can fathom what God has done from beginning to end. ¹² I know that there is nothing better for people than to be happy and to do good while they live. ¹³ That each of them may eat and drink, and find satisfaction in all their toil – this is the gift of God. ¹⁴ I know that everything God does will endure forever; nothing can be added to it and nothing taken from it. God does it so that people will fear him."*

God's will for our lives will, in fact, never change. It is already set. If we choose not to follow God's will, God's plan will adapt, and someone else who is choosing God's plan for their life will receive the inheritance that was originally set for you. God loves us all while we are here on Earth. He loves his children, who are in Heaven. He does not love those who did not receive him, who are in Hell. The conclusion on Ecclesiastes is this (Chapter 12 verses 13–14 NIV):

¹³ Now all has been heard;
here is the conclusion of the matter:
fear God and keep his commandments,
for this is the duty of all mankind.

^{14} For God will bring every deed into judgment,
including every hidden thing,
whether it is good or evil.

A fear of God is healthy. If you are God's elite, God's children, you fear God. You fear God because God is love. God gives us hope for the future. The end of this earth is the hope God's children can rest assured in—that one day, we will be worshipping God in Heaven. An encounter with God, as a human, brings fear. Time after time in the Bible, when people encounter God, physically, their first reaction is fear. God does not want a relationship with us out of fear, but God is the God of justice as well. Everything will come to judgment, good or bad.

Hope has always made me nervous. Hope requires a person to rely strictly on belief or faith. Hope requires that we believe in something that we see as having potential as to happen in the future. Hope requires trust in faith or believing in something unseen. God gives us a plan if we seek Him. God gives us hope. In Philippians 3:12–21 (ESV), Paul explains how he had hope for the future in Christ:

"*^{12} Not that I have already obtained this or am already perfect, but I press on to make it my own, because Christ Jesus has made me his own. ^{13} Brothers, I do not consider that I have made it my own. But one thing I do: forgetting what lies behind and straining forward to what lies ahead, ^{14} I press on toward the goal for the prize of the upward call of God in Christ Jesus. ^{15} Let those of us who are mature think this way, and if in anything you think otherwise, God will reveal that also to you. ^{16} Only let us hold true to what we have attained. ^{17} Brothers, join in imitating me, and keep your eyes on those who walk according to the example you have in us. ^{18} For many, of whom I have often told you and now tell you even with tears, walk as enemies of the cross of Christ. ^{19} Their end is destruction, their god is their belly, and they glory in their shame, with minds set on earthly things. ^{20} But our citizenship is in heaven, and from it we await a Savior, the Lord Jesus Christ, ^{21} who will* *transform our lowly body to be like his glorious body, by the power that enables him even to subject all things to himself."*

Paul, as we all know, had a rough past. He was a follower of the law. He had the perfect pedigree or resume amongst his peers in society. He killed Christians. The latter half of his life was spent improving and advancing the Kingdom of God—the one thing he tried so desperately to destroy before that extreme incident on the Road to Damascus. Paul turned his life around and put his past behind him. He became transformed in Christ Jesus; he put his old ways behind him and was reformed in the ways of God. He had a hope in Christ Jesus in Philippians.

The difference between Paul and Judas is that Paul stopped looking at his past. The Bible never really defines Judas' past, but it does mention he was a crook and remained one until the day he died. It alludes to him not showing any signs of changing. He simply remained what he was. He *chose* to remain what he was. Paul, however, chose to transform into who God had called him to be. He decided to look for a chance of having hope for a better tomorrow. He chose to follow God until the day he died.

Consider this… In Proverbs 16:9 (ESV), Solomon exclaims, *"The heart of man plans his way, but the L*ORD ESTABLISHES HIS STEPS.*"* The idea behind what Solomon is writing to us is simply that we can plan out our lives. We can plan out every single detail about how we expect to live our lives, but God is going to intercede. He is going to "establish our steps" in many ways, shapes, and forms according to His will. Does God give us free will? Yes, God gives us the ability to have a choice in every aspect of our lives. Does God have a plan for your life? Yes, but only if you allow Him to be a part of your life. You must choose to follow God and have a relationship with Him.

I'll take you back to another verse I shared from Proverbs— Proverbs 14:12 (NKJV) *"There is a way that seems right to a man, but in the end leads to death."* In most, if not every situation, we have multiple options in the choices we have to make on a daily basis. There are multiple factors for each one of those choices that can sway our decision one way or another. The Bible talks about taking the road less traveled, implying for simplicity's sake two roads per choice, but typically in any given scenario, there are roads that lead right, left, up, down, diagonal, etc. Roads are leading all over the place! This is the miraculous thing about God: He will let you choose the road you want to go down. He already knows what road you are going to choose, and He uses that for the good of His plan. Life is so much easier when we choose to align our paths with God's plan for our lives.

Take it from me—I have lived my life planning and planning and planning. Ever since I was a child, I had plans for what I wanted to become—occupationally, family life, church life, etc. I have planned so much. We, as humans, plan so much. I will tell you from my life, and I am positive most folks can relate, the plans that I have made that do not align with God's plan for my life typically don't work out, and if they do, then the succeeding activities don't. The plans that I have made that align with God's plan always work out. This is where submission to God's plan has benefitted me the most. One fear I have always had is the fear of not following God's plan in my life. It's a fear of disobeying God and finding myself on the wrong side of Heaven when I die. It is the fear of not completing the race of life. As long as we follow God's word to the best of our ability, and the plan He has for our life to the best of my ability, then our success (which is truly God's success, not ours) will continue to grow and prosper.

Us humans will always plan. It's part of our human nature. It seems to be ingrained in our DNA. We will plan our way, but each way has its own steps. As Proverbs says, God establishes those steps. There are a couple of ways you can look at it. One way would be, of course, to accept God's plan and try to follow His steps for your life as much as possible, knowing that no one is perfect and you won't do everything according to plan. The other option is to plan your own way and attempt to figure out your own steps to fulfill a plan for your life. I will tell you that if you are looking to do God's will and are trying to make it into His presence, in Heaven, your way is not going to work. Sometimes our earthly desires and wants do not align with God's plan.

Matthew 10:5–42 (NIV) explains what Jesus told His chosen disciples about what would happen during their ministries. Imagine getting this news about how your life will be and what God's plan looks like for your life:

"*⁵ These twelve Jesus sent out with the following instructions: 'Do not go among the Gentiles or enter any town of the Samaritans. ⁶ Go rather to the lost sheep of Israel. ⁷ As you go, proclaim this message: "The kingdom of heaven has come near." ⁸ Heal the sick, raise the dead, cleanse those who have leprosy, drive out demons. Freely you have received; freely give. ⁹ Do not get any gold or silver or copper to take with you in your belts—¹⁰ no bag for the journey or extra shirt or sandals or a staff, for the worker is worth his keep. ¹¹ Whatever town or village you enter, search there for some worthy person and stay at their house until you leave. ¹² As you enter the home, give it your greeting. ¹³ If the home is deserving, let your peace rest on it; if it is not, let your peace return to you. ¹⁴ If anyone will not welcome you or listen to your words, leave that home or town and shake the dust off your feet.*

"*¹⁵ Truly I tell you, it will be more bearable for Sodom and Gomorrah on the day of judgment than for that town. ¹⁶ I am sending you out like sheep among wolves. Therefore be as shrewd as snakes and as innocent as doves. ¹⁷ Be on your guard; you will be handed over to the local councils and be flogged in the synagogues. ¹⁸ On my account you will be brought before governors and kings as witnesses to them and to the Gentiles. ¹⁹ But when they arrest you, do not worry about what to say or how to say it. At that time you will be given what to say, ²⁰ for it will not be you speaking, but the Spirit of your Father speaking through you. ²¹ Brother will betray brother to death, and a father his child; children will rebel against their parents and have them put to death. ²² You will be hated by everyone because of me, but the one who stands firm to the end will be saved. ²³ When you are persecuted in one place, flee to another. Truly I tell you, you will not finish going through the towns of Israel before the Son of Man comes. ²⁴ The student is not above the teacher, nor a servant above his master. ²⁵ It is enough for students to be like their teachers, and servants like their masters. If the head of the house has been called*

Beelzebul, how much more the members of his household! ²⁶ *So do not be afraid of them, for there is nothing concealed that will not be disclosed, or hidden that will not be made known.*

"²⁷ What I tell you in the dark, speak in the daylight; what is whispered in your ear, proclaim from the roofs. ²⁸ Do not be afraid of those who kill the body but cannot kill the soul. Rather, be afraid of the One who can destroy both soul and body in hell. ²⁹ Are not two sparrows sold for a penny? Yet not one of them will fall to the ground outside your Father's care. ³⁰ And even the very hairs of your head are all numbered. ³¹ So don't be afraid; you are worth more than many sparrows. ³² Whoever acknowledges me before others, I will also acknowledge before my Father in heaven. ³³ But whoever disowns me before others, I will disown before my Father in heaven. ³⁴ Do not suppose that I have come to bring peace to the earth. I did not come to bring peace, but a sword. ³⁵ For I have come to turn "'a man against his father, a daughter against her mother, a daughter-in-law against her mother-in-law—³⁶ a man's enemies will be the members of his own household.'

"³⁷ Anyone who loves their father or mother more than me is not worthy of me; anyone who loves their son or daughter more than me is not worthy of me. ³⁸ Whoever does not take up their cross and follow me is not worthy of me. ³⁹ Whoever finds their life will lose it, and whoever loses their life for my sake will find it. ⁴⁰ Anyone who welcomes you welcomes me, and anyone who welcomes me welcomes the one who sent me. ⁴¹ Whoever welcomes a prophet as a prophet will receive a prophet's reward, and whoever welcomes a righteous person as a righteous person will receive a righteous person's reward. ⁴² And if anyone gives even a cup of cold water to one of these little ones who is my disciple, truly I tell you, that person will certainly not lose their reward."

The first part of this prophecy seems rather cool. Healing the sick, raising the dead…cool stuff. But then you get to the part about the beatings and public humiliation, which is not so cool. This is where trust in God is a hard pill to swallow, and may turn people away from faith in Jesus Christ. Regardless, God had a plan for the disciples, which was spelled out by Jesus in Matthew

10. The disciples, after hearing this, probably thought, *what have we gotten ourselves into?* Some may have even been deathly afraid. This was the "pep-talk" Jesus gave the disciples before he was betrayed and executed. This was the "pep-talk" He gave to anyone who chose to follow Him. There is fear in the unknown. Jesus was telling His disciples, His followers, "I know what is going to happen to you." He lays it out in this scripture and gives us the choice to follow. At the point when someone has to say, "don't be afraid" in any circumstance, you know there is something that is going to be worth fearing to some extent. I'm not saying we should actually be afraid; you just know there is going to be some challenges. With any challenges comes some sort of fear. Fear may drive separation from God's plan. Love opposes fear. It is love that drives us towards God's plan for our lives.

It's that true godly love that sets God's children apart from the rest of the world. It's not statistics or works alone. Love is the key to unlocking God's will for our lives. If we cannot see how God loves, then how can we be a friend of God's? How can we be one of His children or chosen ones, if we cannot show His love to others? We must love God, and we must love others. In loving others, we are also showing love to God because God loves all people. We love God by fearing Him and keeping His commandments. We love God by pressing on in this world, not looking to the past for answers but striving forward to the future and what's to come of us in the final days. We love God through trusting Him and the hope He has given us as His children. I'll let you in on a little secret: the good guys win. I'm not a competitive person per se, but in this case, it's all about winning.

Chosen. Let that word sink into your thoughts and stop questioning God's intentions for your life. Simply live. Simply be. We can forgive ourselves and we can forgive others. The most important part of loving is forgiveness.

Are we destined to succeed or fail? The Bible almost seems to go back and forth on this topic. In the faith of Christianity, the Bible is the inspired word of God. Meaning, though written by a number of people (humans), God has His hand on every word.

We could go into a history lesson on why each book of the Bible was chosen to be put in the traditional Bible we know today, but at this point, it's water under the bridge. The message of Jesus Christ is the message God wants every individual to receive. That is the true message the Bible proclaims. Romans 8:28–30 (NIV) explains how we can look at being chosen:

"[28] And we know that in all things God works for the good of those who love him, who have been called according to his purpose. [29] For those God foreknew he also predestined to be conformed to the image of his Son, that he might be the firstborn among many brothers and sisters. [30] And those he predestined, he also called; those he called, he also justified; those he justified, he also glorified."

As we believe in that message, knowing whether or not we are predestined or predetermined in this life is scary to think about. It's disturbing by some means because control is an attribute folks do not like to let go of in life. The Bible tells us in Proverbs 3:5–6 (NIV) to *"Trust in the Lord with all your heart and lean not on your own understanding; in all your ways submit to him, and he will make your paths straight."* Submission is hard. It is an act of release from oneself and the ways in which one thinks, acts, and lives. This verse in Proverbs tells us that if we put our trust in God, if we submit to God, He will direct our paths.

There are other verses in the Bible that allude to our lives being planned out. God's plan. In that sense, we have destiny. We can only find our true destiny by submitting to and by trusting in God. God has shown us who He is in His word. Please do not take this as blasphemous, but it would seem that putting one's trust in someone they cannot see is not logical, but it is the individual's choice to believe or not believe that the deity (God) is all-knowing, all-powerful, all-present, and loves them. The Bible gives us the answers we long for in life. We don't know exactly how life will turn out and what our true destiny is until we reach the end of what's to come.

There have only been a few people throughout history that have known their destiny ahead of time. Maybe. To us "common" folk, we can't know what our lives will entail until we get there.

By then, our destiny will be history. Frustrating? Yes, but such is life. If we knew it all before it happened, would it be enjoyable? You know us humans, we would definitely try to change things before they occurred. Then we would be equal to God in some ways. Can you imagine how the world would be if we had a bunch of imperfect beings (humans) running around playing God? As Solomon puts it in Ecclesiastes 9:11–12 (NIV), there is too much *"time and chance"* that we live through to control everything. These verse read:

> *"11* I have seen something else under the sun:
>
> *The race is not to the swift*
> *or the battle to the strong,*
> *nor does food come to the wise*
> *or wealth to the brilliant*
> *or favor to the learned;*
> *but time and chance happen to them all.*
>
> *12 Moreover, no one knows when their hour will come:*
>
> *As fish are caught in a cruel net,*
> *or birds are taken in a snare,*
> *so people are trapped by evil times*
> *that fall unexpectedly upon them."*

We will never be able to fathom God's plan and its entirety. With every action on this planet, there is a shift in "the plan." God does give us choice. So that means, on a daily basis, each individual on this planet is making thousands, if not hundreds of thousands, of decisions. With that said, how many different scenarios could play out just in a single second? Currently, there are probably seven to eight billion people on the planet. Countless scenarios for that many people, all at the same time. This may be hard to hear for some of you. I know it's hard for me to take in. We must trust in God out of survival. We do not have the capacity to even begin to fathom how "complete" destiny even works. To quote the band Linkin Park, "In the end, it doesn't even matter."

The Bible tells us that Moses was the writer of the 90th Psalm (at least that's what the subtitle says, not the actual scripture). I'm not sure exactly when this psalm was written, but I believe it was written after Moses realized he would not be entering into the Promised Land. I could be wrong, but just a hunch. Regardless, he touches on the point that this life is not the endpoint of eternity. We come into this world, we live, and then we die. Psalm 90 speaks of the concept of "numbering our days." Moses, in the book of Numbers, chapter 10, was commanded by God to speak to a rock to have water come from it. Instead, he struck it with his rod, and in that moment, his rebellion was the reason God would not allow him to enter into the Promised Land God had set aside for the Israelites. When Moses hit the rock, he was angry with the people for doubting God so much. This miracle took place towards the end of the 40-year period they had spent wandering around the desert; I'm sure tensions were running a little high at that point. As Moses did not enter the Promised Land, he was able to see it from across the Jordan River (not to be confused with the "Jordan Riedel"). Sorry…the point I want to make is that "we must learn to number our days" (Psalm 90 NIV).

> "[1] Lord, you have been our dwelling place
> *throughout all generations.*
> [2] Before the mountains were born
> *or you brought forth the whole world,*
> *from everlasting to everlasting you are God.*
> [3] You turn people back to dust,
> *saying, 'Return to dust, you mortals.'*
> [4] A thousand years in your sight
> *are like a day that has just gone by,*
> *or like a watch in the night.*
> [5] Yet you sweep people away in the sleep of death—
> *they are like the new grass of the morning:*
> [6] In the morning it springs up new,

> *but by evening it is dry and withered.*
> *⁷ We are consumed by your anger*
> *and terrified by your indignation.*
> *⁸ You have set our iniquities before you,*
> *our secret sins in the light of your presence.*
> *⁹ All our days pass away under your wrath;*
> *we finish our years with a moan.*
> *¹⁰ Our days may come to seventy years,*
> *or eighty, if our strength endures;*
> *yet the best of them are but trouble and sorrow,*
> *for they quickly pass, and we fly away.*
> *¹¹ If only we knew the power of your anger!*
> *Your wrath is as great as the fear that is your due.*
> *¹² Teach us to number our days,*
> *that we may gain a heart of wisdom."*

When we number our days, we gain wisdom. With wisdom comes a whole slew of things. For example: self-control, patience, and so on. With time, we become better people—better Christ followers. God sometimes humbles us when we need it the most, and when His plan calls for it. In Moses' case, he was humbled by God. Reading the book of Numbers, it seems like his anger with how the people of Israel had been acting for the last 40 years in the desert was just getting to him. Coupled alongside a little entitlement (maybe), God's plan was for Moses to be humbled. If we get to that point in our lives where we feel like we are acting, instead of God acting through us, you can be assured that God will humble you. Anyway, that's a lesson for another time. Learn to number your days. Days will come, and they will go. We must remember to look at our days as a tiny moment in time and that God has a larger plan that is never-ending.

The last book of the Bible is Revelations. If you truly want to know what happens at the end of time on this planet, read it. I would encourage you to read it, but just know that some parts are kind of weird in imagining how the Prophet John's description will play out. Just know, one day this world will end. Our time as being humans will end. There will be an end. These moments here on Earth are just a blip in eternity. You can choose to be on the right side of Heaven. You can choose where you spend eternity. You can choose God's will over your own. Eternity goes on, regardless of what you choose and what others choose. You can only make decisions for yourself, no one else. That is why the Bible tells us that one day, we will stand before the judgment thrown…on our own, with only ourselves to look at.

It is your choice to make. God's will or your own? If you decide to choose the correct path of your destiny (God's path), God will be there for you. It's your destiny to make this choice—your life and your soul depend on it. Your eternity depends on it. Heaven or Hell? God or man? You choose. Will you be God's CHOSEN?

> *"[16] This is what the LORD SAYS—*
> *he who made a way through the sea,*
> *a path through the mighty waters,*
> *[17] who drew out the chariots and horses,*
> *the army and reinforcements together,*
> *and they lay there, never to rise again,*
> *extinguished, snuffed out like a wick:*
> *[18] Forget the former things;*
> *do not dwell on the past.*
> *[19] See, I am doing a new thing!*
> *Now it springs up; do you not perceive it?*
> *I am making a way in the wilderness*
> *and streams in the wasteland.*
> *[20] The wild animals honor me,*
> *the jackals and the owls,*
> *because I provide water in the wilderness*
> *and streams in the wasteland,*
> *to give drink to my people, my chosen,*
> *[21] the people I formed for myself*
> *that they may proclaim my praise."*
> Isaiah 43:16–21 (NIV)

www.ingramcontent.com/pod-product-compliance
Lightning Source LLC
Chambersburg PA
CBHW070122110526
44587CB00017BA/3099